"Nothing is more frightening than the thought of parenting a teenager in today's culture! Mr. Ezzo and Dr. Bucknam's book will show parents of today's preteens that it is possible to have a great relationship with their children during those years by applying timeless principles they may have forgotten."

DOUG GILMAN, YOUTH PASTOR
HILTON HEAD ISLAND, SC

"A resource like this is priceless. *On Becoming Preteen Wise* will encourage parents and challenge them to apply its principles. The authors set a high standard for the family and give practical suggestions about how to live out that standard. Each chapter covers a critical issue that I see parents grappling with. I use the processes and techniques in my practice to move families toward health and in my own family to ensure the best outcomes for our family of five."

LINDA G. ALLEN, M.A., ATR EXPRESSIVE THERAPIST,
COUNSELOR AT SOUTHEAST CHRISTIAN CHURCH, LOUISVILLE, KY

"Here is a wonderful resource to help parents move toward the relational goal of true friendship with their children. The principles contained within *On Becoming Preteen Wise* can help any parent build a firm foundation, establish a healthy family identity, and help avoid the future tension of teenage rebellion."

ELSIE WOOLF, M.A. MARRIAGE AND FAMILY COUNSELOR

"As a pediatric cardiologist, I treat the hearts of young people from infancy through the teen years. I can keep them alive with medicine. *On Becoming PreTeen Wise* is the medicine I prescribe to their parents to keep the entire family healthy."

PENN LAIRD, M.D., PEDIATRIC CARDIOLOGIST

ON BECOMING

PRETEEN

WISE

Parenting Your Child from
Eight to Twelve Years

GARY EZZO, M.A. AND
ROBERT BUCKNAM, M.D.

PARENT-WISE SOLUTIONS

ON BECOMING PRETEEN WISE
(Parenting you child from eight to twelve)

® "ON BECOMING" is a registered trademark

Parentwise Solutions Inc,
(A Division of the Charleston Publishing Group, Inc.)

Cover photograph by Portlock Productions

Printed in the United States of America

Parent-Wise Solutions, Inc.
Administrative Offices
2160 Cheswick Lane
Mount Pleasant, SC 29466

Print Run/Year
4-10   5-11   6-12   7-14

Dedicated To:

Ron and Kathy Seidel

Compassionate friends touching heaven, touching earth

TABLE OF CONTENTS

ACKNOWLEDGMENTS

We are indebted to a host of friends who have influenced the writing of this book. Among them are John and Holly Angle, Greg and Diane Roehr, Kim and Kathy Lambros, Robert Boerman, and Jeff and Sharon Secor. A special thanks to Anne Marie Ezzo for her contribution of chapter fourteen.

FOREWORD

A small woman huddled on the floor in the parenting section of a trendy bookstore. Frantically, she searched the titles at ankle level. "Don't worry. You can step on me," she said to a shopper headed her way. "It probably wouldn't phase me." The passerby, who noticed the woman's puffy eyes and disheveled appearance, discreetly asked the frazzled woman if she was suffering from allergies. "No," she said, "My nine-year-old just told me to get out of his life. So, I picked up my bag and came here."

Here. To the answer mecca of the universe: the bookstore. To find yet another book on how to handle her nine-year-old. Yet, she left empty-handed. After skimming the childbirth and first-year sections and looking through those oh-so-encouraging torturous-twos volumes, she undoubtedly noticed a major leap. Suddenly she landed in the teen section, which put forth countless theories on dealing with troublesome teens and their painful problems like bulimia and body piercing.

As for books on the family, she may have noticed titles such as *The Vegetarian Child, Carbohydrate-Addicted Kids, Children with Work Inhibitions,* and *Children of Third Marriages.* Nope. Nothing here. No hope. No clues—only the inference that this woman could meet her perceived needs with a good cup of java. She has plenty of time. According to the shelves, there's a whole four years till she really needs help.

Trying to find a book written about children living in the

growth-packed years between the ages of eight and twelve can be an eerie experience. Why the literary silence? If your experience is like ours, you may have to ask the manager for some help. We recently visited seven major book dealers within a three mile radius of our home: a Super Crown, two B. Daltons, one Barnes and Noble, one Waldenbooks, and two Christian bookstores.

Amazingly, not one of these stores carried a single book written specifically about parenting a child through the middle years. The closest we found was a few random volumes of the Gesell Institute of Human Development series by Dr. Louise Ames. Even these titles were limited to one-year periods of development.

Why such a dearth of information on the middle years? One possible explanation lies in the character of our society, which seems very willing to spend time and money to fix its problems, but very little of either to prevent them. When we are in a crisis, we have incredible resolve to find solutions for our problems. If we had the same resolve to prevent those crises, we might avoid many trials and much pain.

This book is based on the familiar axiom that an ounce of prevention is worth a pound of cure. It's much easier to avoid making mistakes that it is to correct them after the fact. This is particularly true of parenting. Just ask any mother or father continually challenged by a contentious or rebellious teen: Given a choice to go back and start over, would you work toward prevention or maintain the status quo and manage in a crisis? It is our firm conviction that rightly meeting the small challenges of the middle years significantly reduces the likelihood of big challenges in the teen years. In other words, the groundwork you lay today will impact your relationship with your children in their teens and even long after they're grown. Therefore this book is as much about building a strong relationship with your middle-years child now as it is about preventing serious teen-parent conflicts in the future.

I can confidently tell you that close, intimate family relationships don't have to end when your children hit adolescence. On the contrary, parents and children can establish a healthy relational foundation that will see them through the teen years and beyond. The best time to do so is now, during the critically important middle years. This book is a deposit on that return.

Before moving any farther, there are three matters to discuss. First, when clinicians talk about preadolescence, or the preteen years, they are generally referring to children between the ages of ten and twelve. This book, however, includes children who are eight and nine years old. This is because the hormonal changes experienced by preadolescents actually begin by age eight. To stay consistent with contemporary terminology, Gary and I will use the word *preteen* when referring to ten- to twelve-year-old children, but we will refer to the broader five-year period, ages eight to twelve, as *the middle years*.

Second, throughout this book we refer to our previous book, *On Becoming Childwise*. There we laid down certain principles that are very applicable to this subsequent stage of growth and development. We have adapted some core strategies from *Childwise* for use in this book.

Third, we would like to acknowledge and thank Anne Marie Ezzo for her wonderful contribution to chapter 14. As a nurse, childbirth instructor, and mother, her practical insights and gentle, conversational style put moms at ease with preparing their daughters for biological maturation and communicating the all-important message about the journey to womanhood.

Now it's time to begin the process of growing together through the middle years. If I have learned anything from my pediatric practice and my own children it is this: The middle years, even more than the teen years, are crucial for preparing a child for responsible adult living. The fifteen hundred days of preadolescence are all the time you have to prepare your kids for the nearly thirty-seven hundred days of adolescence.

Let's make the most of every minute.

ROBERT BUCKNAM, M.D.

LOUISVILLE, COLORADO

INTRODUCTION

Imagine a NASA spacecraft on its way to Mars. Assuming the ground controllers and on-board navigation systems have done their jobs correctly, the lander should be in the general vicinity of the red planet when it's time to think about landing. There are several phases in the flight toward the Martian rendezvous. Right up until that last moment there are opportunities for course corrections. But at some point, the controllers have to just let go and trust that the mechanisms and software will get the craft safely to the surface.

Raising a child is a lot like sending a spacecraft to Mars. Your job as a parent of a small child (up to age 7) is to install everything the child will need for his long journey toward adulthood. The middle years (8–12) are like the cruise stage—everything from escaping Earth's atmosphere to arriving in Mars's orbit. During these years you'll be calling on the systems you placed aboard your little craft, using them to make course corrections as the moment of truth draws near. That's what this book is about—helping you land a child safely in the teen years.

The success of any landing is often determined by the little course corrections made just before the lander starts its decent. In teen parenting those course corrections come during the critical middle years between eight and twelve. This is not the time for parents to take a mental time-out.

Once the child enters the free fall of the teenage atmosphere, parents have to sit back and hope that all the work they've done and all the tools they've equipped their little lander with will be sufficient to see him through. Are you prepared? Understand, there is plenty of hope for a successful landing because the middle years provide needed time for significant course corrections.

During the preteen years, your child will be changing. He will no longer communicate in the same way he did previously. Relationships with peers will not be the same. What the group thinks will become important. Members of the opposite sex will start looking less icky. His body will change.

But the middle-years child isn't the only one who is changing. This is a transition for the parents, too. Parents have to walk through each of these transitions with the child. And the style of parenting has to change. No longer can parents lead primarily through authority. The style of parenting that works with teens is *influence*. It is during the preteen years that parents have to change their "because Mommy said so" style of parenting—which was often appropriate when the child was younger—to a style that promotes and exemplifies self-governing, responsible behavior guided by internal self-control.

Take a deep breath. We'll guide you through what parenting should look like during this major period of growth. Sit back and enjoy this book. We are positive you will find courage for your parenting.

Prepare for launch.

TRANSITIONS

Chapter One

Middle-Years Transitions

*L*et's face it: Your child is changing. She doesn't watch Barney anymore. She doesn't want your help quite as much. Her emotions are exaggerated. And she's suddenly realized that not everyone is her friend just because they're in the same class together. She's begun dealing with deeply felt issues like freedom, friendship, peer approval—even fashion.

Wait! Maybe you're not ready for this. You're still quite comfortable setting out Disney plates and chicken nuggets. Now she wants tossed salad with low-cal dressing?

Your middle-years child is changing.

WHO'S TRAINING WHOM?

At one of our parenting conferences, a frazzled mother of two middle-years children confessed to the audience: "My children bring out the worst in me."

"Yes," Gary responded. "That's exactly what children do to parents. They expose us for who we are and what we know. They also expose us for who we're not and what we don't know."

We all know that parenting is a process that leads to maturity, but what we don't always realize is that the children aren't the only ones maturing. Because middle-years children are grappling with right and wrong in new ways, parents are forced to evaluate their own moral code. When children repeatedly test parents' boundaries, it develops patience and conviction in the parents. Parents have to gain verbal self-control because effective parenting cannot be explosive, critical, or sarcastic. Our children reveal the weaknesses of our character and the areas in which we need to mature.

So this chapter starts with you, Mom and Dad. Your moral growth as a parent is hardly an option. Few of us enter parenting with a full grasp of life's virtues, but the demand for moral wisdom in parenting has never been so great. Why is that? Every major moral mandate—love, mercy, grace, justice, humility, forgiveness, restoration, compassion, patience, and self-control, to name a few—is challenged in parenting, often daily!

The parenting process forces moms and dads to mature in a way no other life experience can. This is a good thing. Parenting provides the ideal circumstance in which we can learn, for no one else in the world will be as forgiving of our shortcomings as our own children. Realizing we do indeed fall short helps us grow in grace toward the children we train.

As a parent, you can't completely avoid making mistakes. Accept it. The best you can do is to study your children, learn from your mistakes, and focus wisely on their upbringing. If not now in the middle years, when? Even in today's investment-savvy society, parents easily miss the mark here, content to coast through the seemingly uneventful middle years. Perhaps they feel they are saving up their strength for the teenage battles ahead. With that approach, they can count on having many.

The teen years don't have to be tumultuous. Understanding the transitions your middle-years children are undergoing will help you all get through their adolescence alive, sane, and closer than ever.

MIDDLE-YEARS TRANSITION: ARRIVALS AND DEPARTURES

There is not a major airport in the United States that Gary and Anne Marie Ezzo have not passed through at least once. Forty weeks a year, they travel from their home in California to one or more cities around the world to lead parenting seminars. They understand the potential difficulties associated with fixed airline schedules. They know what it is like to arrive in a city, deplane, rush to find the next gate, and be off again.

Happily, the airlines know the potential for passengers to lose their way in transit. That is why they have uniformed agents waiting at the gate to help passengers in need of connecting flight information. These agents direct passengers from where they are to where they need to be.

During your child's middle years, one of your primary functions is to play the role of gate agent. As your child arrives from a wide range of childhood experiences, your job is to point him in the right direction and, in some cases, to lead the way. This means that you, yourself, must have a clear picture of where your child should be headed.

For example, perhaps your son watches a movie with a nasty villain and a surprisingly respectable teen hero. To your disappointment, your boy seems more enamored with the villain and takes on the cool tones and hardened gaze of this unlikely role model. Time for the gate agent to step in. Your son needs assistance with his baggage—emotional and otherwise—and guidance to a more desirable destination.

The middle years is a period of great transition—a developmental phase when a child moves from where he has been to where he needs to go. During this phase of growth, you are still his first choice as a guide, and he needs your leadership. Take advantage of that. Below are eight critical middle-years transitions. Help him through them well, and the next leg of the journey just might be crash-free.

1. Transitioning away from Childhood and Childhood Structures

On the first day of kindergarten, you followed her bus all the way to school just to make sure she remembered to get off, that she was smiling when she did, or that she didn't evaporate in the few miles from here to there. You laughed; you cried; you chatted with the other half-dozen teary adults who all did the same silly thing.

Guess what? It's time to back off. From now on, wave good-bye from the porch.

Finding relational equilibrium with your maturing child is one of the more difficult tasks of parenthood. But by the end of this growth period, a healthy restructuring of relationships needs to have occurred for both you and your child.

This isn't your four-year-old anymore. This is a young person on the verge of adolescence. You need to begin treating her like a responsible individual. You may be surprised to find that's what she has actually become.

During the middle years, children begin the long process of metamorphosis toward healthy independence. They move away from childhood structures, dependencies, and interests. There is a shift from a world centered largely around relationships with Mom, Dad, and siblings, to a world in which relationships with peers, friends, and real heroes begin to draw their focus.

This particular transition is demonstrated by the way a child attempts to distance himself from early childhood structures. While certain terminology didn't bother your child at age five or six, at eight or nine that same boy or girl will object to conversations that describe him or her in childhood phrases such as "He's my little guy" or "Yes, she's my princess."

Young Ryan couldn't wait for his week at camp the summer he was nine. Upon arrival, he began unpacking the tidy bundle his mom had prepared. To his horror, he discovered the pillowcase. There was Superman striking a bold pose, much to his campmates' delight. Ryan's week at camp turned into one very long bad dream. The endless ribbing left him wishing he could disappear into a phone booth.

At eight or nine, your child has already done an enormous amount of learning. Contrast him with the nearly helpless toddler of a few years ago who needed the structure of Mom and Dad's direct companionship, love, and supervision. A guiding parent or other supervising adult orchestrated all wake time, naptime, mealtime, and playtime. Your child's friends were limited to the kids in the neighborhood or his playgroups. Your child lived in a world predominately structured and made secure by you.

Consider the child who at five held your hand everywhere you went and at six advanced to crossing the street by herself. Now, she is notably less dependent on you and the sheltering structures you created for her protection (and your comfort). A driving sense of her own self-sufficiency is replacing your preadolescent's long-standing preoccupation with personal caretakers.

Early in the middle-years transition, children begin to reject all sorts of minor childhood-related associations that they previously found comforting. The little girl who once was consoled after an injury by sitting on Mom's lap may start going to her siblings for comfort instead. The young boy who once would not go anywhere without his stuffed animal now buries it in his closet toy box. This is just the beginning.

2. Transitioning to Knowing the Facts

"You're out! I touched the base."

"No, I'm not! You have to touch *me*."

They can barely swing the bat, but they brandish their knowledge of the rules as if they had a deep and abiding understanding of the game.

Your middle-years child now relates to other children as peers and to other adults as something more than parental substitutes. During this period boys and girls demonstrate a need to organize, categorize, and play by the rules. It is important to them that they get their facts right (although they have an oversimplified notion of the correctness of their own assessment during this phase).

Perhaps you're having a conversation with another adult in which you describe an incident that occurred at the store today. You aren't even two sentences into your story when you hear from the only other eyewitness to the event, your nine-year-old daughter. "No, Mom, that's not how it happened. The man with the shopping cart bumped the manager and then...."

Don't be surprised when your attempt to abbreviate a conversation is met by a challenge from your middle-years child, who suddenly seems to have a desperate need to get the story right, as if one fact out of sequence will cause the universe to instantly implode.

Now add birth order to this mix. Because the eldest is born into a world of adults and not siblings, she tends to have an increased need to be "right" about all things. If another child breaks the rules, she is relentless in her efforts to straighten that child out or bring justice to bear on a situation. "Mom! That's not fair! When I was Billy's age, you never let me ride to the corner by myself." Look for these verbal declarations—they're all part of the transition process.

3. Transitioning from Imagination to Reason

With the middle years comes a distinct shift toward logical thinking. Logic and reason now help your child to begin overcoming the unknown.

Consider how small children deal with fear of the unknown or unexplained circumstances. A nighttime shadow on the bedroom wall becomes the villain from their favorite action film. A loud noise in the distance is a monster on its way to the house! Because their imaginations develop more rapidly than their reasoning skills, and because they're aware of their own smallness, younger children often interpret anything they don't understand as something to be feared.

But everything changes during the middle years. Reason rises to challenge imagination. This means your eight-year-old will begin to appear more daring and adventuresome and less restrained by fear of the unknown.

4. Transitioning to New Emotional Patterns and Expressions

Every healthy child comes into this life with the potential for experiencing the full range of human emotions. Obviously, these emotions influence the way we think and act.

Though all humans have the same emotions, each of us responds to these feelings differently. Some responses are constructive; others are detrimental. In the latter case, it is not the emotions themselves that get us into trouble, but the manner in which we deal with them.

The more we respond to an emotion in a certain way, the greater the likelihood that it will develop into a habit. Developing positive habits is particularly important during the middle years because this is the season of life in which a child's moral knowledge (moral truth taught by parents and teachers), combined with his emotions, can help establish patterns of right behavior.

For example, the child who learns early in life that "honesty is the best policy" is likely to carry that teaching into adulthood. Your four-year-old can understand the principle, but your eight-year-old can make it a way of life.

Do not miss this important point: You and your home environment will play a dominant role in shaping your child's profile of emotional responses, especially during the middle years. A child who observes Dad returning wrong for wrong by walking the dog on a neighbor's lawn as payback for a similar disservice will learn that paybacks are okay for peers. If right responses are not learned during the middle years, wrong ones will most likely characterize the teen years. Now is when you need to check out your own attitudes.

The middle years also bring about a shift in a child's outward expression of emotions. A young child's emotional outburst lasts a few minutes, and then it's over. Contrast this response with that of the socially sensitive middle-years child whose short-lived outbursts have given way to drawn-out periods of moodiness.

What all this demonstrates is that your middle-years child can now exercise cognitive control over his emotions. A few years earlier, this was not the case. The decision of how to behave is, in the end, your child's. However, you still play a significant role in shaping how your child develops his or her responses. Take advantage of this.

5. *Transitioning to Hormone-Activated Bodies*

Perhaps you have found yourself thinking, "My child is only eight or nine—it can't be hormones yet." Yes, it can. Most people think hormonal changes don't begin until just before a child reaches the teen years, when they naturally set into motion a series of defiant acts and rebellious mood swings.

But the truth is that hormonal changes in a child's endocrine system begin at approximately age seven, not twelve or thirteen. You may have already begun to see the effects.

Yes, your middle-years child is hormonally active. From this point on, he or she will experience greater emotional highs and lows. This may, in turn, affect behavior. But wait: The fact that your child is undergoing these changes does not provide an excuse for wrong behavior.

Have you ever wondered why your nine-year-old daughter can change moods overnight? She may go through phases of discouragement and break into tears over minor details. Someone looked at her wrong. She looks all wrong. She's not sure what is wrong. Her face becomes a little oilier, and she is sure everyone is noticing. For a few days she becomes more snippety toward her siblings. Then, just as quickly, she returns to being the stable child you knew before. Hormones at work.

While hormones play their part, the moral environment in which your child is raised also plays a significant role in shaping her perception of her changing body and the sexual tension natural to growth. Clinicians have noted that children who come from differing domestic moral climates will have very different sensual experiences.

For example, young girls weaned on MTV are more likely to express their budding sense of womanhood according to the images promoted by the sexual image-makers of MTV. In contrast, pubescent daughters coming from homes that do not allow this influence tend to direct their budding sexual awareness into channels of innocent romantic thought.

Have your ever watched *Anne of Green Gables* and *Anne of Avonlea*? It took Anne, the main character of this drama, eight hours (in film time—eight years in story time) to realize that it was Gilbert, her old school chum, she really loved. While such romantic portrayals are entertaining for a sixty-year-old woman and perhaps confusing for a six-year-old girl, a ten-year-old girl enters into eight hours of romance by identifying herself with the heroine.

Why is she hooked, while her six-year-old female cousin and her eleven-year-old brother find something else to do? Because hormones active in her body have brought about a burgeoning sense of romance. Her body awakens her mind to a vague but real awareness that someday perhaps there will be a Gilbert for her, too.

Endocrine changes awaken a sense of romantic sensitivity in girls much earlier than they do in boys. Your ten-year-old daughter is asking: "Mom, how did you and Dad meet?" or "Where did you go on your first date?" Meanwhile, a boy of the same age is asking, "Mom, have you seen my football?"

Valiant knights prance their white steeds dreamily through your daughter's thoughts. But it will be another year or two before the neighbor boy of the same age starts to consider your daughter more than a decent right fielder or someone to torment with his plastic spider. But in time, preteen boys, too, succumb to the powerful effect of hormones on their views of the opposite sex.

6. Transitioning to the Growing Influence of Peers

The middle years are marked by a greater sensitivity to the differences between self and peers. Any slight deviation in growth or secondary sex characteristics from what is common in the group will cause the middle-years child to worry.

Such an occurrence is natural and quite unavoidable. The

young girl who begins to develop prematurely will measure herself against other girls. The boy who starts to show hairs on his chin or to grow disproportionately in height will become self-conscious about his differences.

This awareness leads to a growing interest in the opinions of others in a child's peer group. *What is the group wearing, listening to, doing? Where are they going? And what does all this mean to me?* There is a fuller discussion of peer involvement, relationships, and influence in chapter 10. For now it is enough to say that the effects of this transition will be felt for quite some time.

7. *Transitioning to a Sense of Morality*

Morality is more than a checklist of good choices one makes in the interest of preserving self. Moral maturity means considering others— respecting the feelings, needs, hurts, and hearts of those with whom the child interacts.

We believe that clearly defined morality is the only foundation upon which healthy relationships and strong families are built. Only moral maturity enables us to get along rightly with others in our families and communities.

Because the middle years are typically far less traumatic than the "terrible twos" or the tumultuous teens, parents tend not to have a sense of moral urgency during this time. Yet if there is ever a time of ripening when a child seeks moral knowledge, it is during these precious middle years. This is the time when you as a parent can encourage and shape the development of moral consciousness in your child.

During the middle years, children not only understand the wider scope of moral truth, they can begin to use it to regulate their lives. Soon they will be able to conform their outward behavior voluntarily, apart from the fear of reproof that so often accompanies a younger child's moral decision-making process. The middle years are when your child will strike deep moral roots—for good or ill—with or without your guidance.

Younger children live off Mom and Dad's values. But during the middle years, children begin to take personal ownership of their values. Are you ready to help your child make the transition?

8. Transitioning from Being Reminded to Being Responsible

The middle years are a time when your child should be transitioning from simply obeying the rules, on the one hand, to taking personal responsibility for tasks, chores, and behavior, on the other. When only obedience is at stake, your child will comply when reminded. When responsibility comes into play, your child does the right thing without being reminded.

As soon as a middle-years child understands what you're asking of her, she should be expected to take ownership of that behavior. This may be a change for her and you. If you don't make it a priority to teach her self-generated initiative now, you'll still be asking if she's done all her homework and picked up her room when she's in college. In the pages that follow, we'll show you how to teach your middle-years children to take the initiative.

The Ninth Transition

There is one more transition to make during the middle years. This one is for parents: Parents of a preadolescent must make the transition from parenting by authority to parenting by influence.

This may be the most important transition of all. Therefore we have devoted all of chapter 3 to it.

SUMMARY

The middle years are a time of realignment and sometimes course correction for children and parents. These are transition years when children start the long process of metamorphosis—moving away from childhood dependencies and interests, toward healthy independence and self-responsibility. It is a period marked by a greater sensitivity to the differences between self and peers and thus by a growing interest in peer approval, which can lead to peer pressure.

The endocrine system begins to release potent hormones which nudge boys and girls toward sexual awareness. Now, boys and girls begin to change their minds about the opposite sex and start to view the other gender as something attractive. Your son or daughter will begin to pay more attention to physical hygiene and personal grooming, including hairstyle and dress.

The middle years mark a time of great moral and intellectual growth in children. Logical thinking and a new capacity for moral understanding are the two prerequisites they need in order to regulate their own behavior in the future. At this time they begin to take ownership of their own values and beliefs. It is a time when the world opens up to them and the meaning of life beyond Mom and Dad's design begins to take shape. It is a time of great transition for your child—and for you.

BRINGING IT HOME

1. What is a middle-years transition?

2. How are you like an airline gate agent in your child's life?

3. How might your family's moral environment help shape your child's perception of his or her changing body and the sexual tension naturally felt during this growth phase?

4. How are hormonal changes in a middle-years child related to the importance of peers?

5. Describe the transition that occurs in relation to morality during the middle years.

Chapter Two

Where Are We Now?

This chapter is composed of two parts: test and explanation. The test is designed to help you see how many of the signs of health your family exhibits. The explanation is to give you an early heads-up about some warning flags that can start to wave during the middle years. Take a moment to work through and score the survey below. Do so for each middle-years child in your family. Then read the discussion that follows.

THE MIDDLE-YEARS TEST

Write in your responses on the blanks adjacent to each question in this section. Rate the questions using a 5-to-1 scale.

5 Always true; i.e., this is very representative of our child, his or her feelings, our feelings, or our relationship.

4 Often the case; i.e., this is usually representative of our child, his or her feelings, our feelings, or our relationship.

3 Sometimes this is true, but just as often it is not.

2 This happens, but not often; i.e., this is not usually representative of our child, his or her feelings, our feelings, or our relationship.

1 This is rarely, if ever, true of our child or our relationship.

_4_ If our preadolescent were at a neighbor's house, and there were a questionable television program or movie on, he or she would either call home to find out if it was okay to watch or would decide not to watch the program.

_5_ Some preadolescents seem to have split personalities, acting one way when with parents, but not yielding to authority at school or church. Our child is not like that.

_4_ For his or her age, our preadolescent avoids troubling situations on his or her own initiative.

_2_ Our preadolescent doesn't make impetuous decisions, but considers future consequences.

_5_ Our preadolescent looks forward to special family times when the family is alone together.

_3_ Our preadolescent doesn't do something good simply to get out of doing what he or she was told.

_1_ Our preadolescent can accept no for an answer without blowing up. He or she doesn't challenge us with a series of "whys?"

_4_ Our preadolescent doesn't tell us a partial truth or openly lie to us instead of admitting irresponsibility.

_5_ Our preadolescent knows that if we wrong him or her in any way, he or she can count on an apology from us.

_2_ Our child doesn't buck the system or demand to do it his or her own way.

_2_ Our preadolescent doesn't take advantage of siblings.

_5_ Some parents don't trust their preadolescents alone at home, even if they are just going next door or will be gone for only an hour. Thank goodness that's not the case with our preadolescent.

_5_ In our family, we practice seeking true forgiveness from one another rather than just saying, "I'm sorry."

_5_ Our preadolescent tends to be drawn to good kids who stay out of trouble instead of to kids who are always getting in trouble.

_5_ Our child tends to enjoy his or her own family more than friends. He or she is not always asking to bring a friend along on family activities.

_2_ Our preadolescent is characterized by self-generated initiative, meaning that when our child sees something that needs to be done, he or she does it.

_2_ Our preadolescent doesn't get jealous or pout when something good happens to a sibling but not to him or her.

_5_ The peers our child is attracted to come from families that share our values.

_5_ Our preadolescent is characterized by the same level of behavior outside our presence as well as when he or she is with us.

_5_ We are so glad to be able to be loosening instead of tightening the boundaries now that our child is in the middle years.

_4_ We're not hearing similar negative reports about our child from various people.

_4_ If our preadolescent has been in trouble while away from us, he or she will come and tell us before we find out from someone else.

_5_ We are pleased to see that our child's attitudes are impacted more by the positive influence of family than by the negative influence of peers.

_5_ We know preadolescents who continually seek attention from the opposite sex, even though it is often done playfully. Our child does not act this way.

_1_ We don't have to remind our preadolescent to pick up after himself or herself.

_1_ Our child, upon receiving the answer no from one parent, doesn't go ask the same question of the second parent without saying that the first has already said no.

_1_ If our preadolescent sees a piece of paper on the floor, even if he or she didn't drop it, he or she will normally pick it up.

_1_ When we ask our preadolescent to do something, we don't end up in a power struggle with him or her.

_5_ At this age our preadolescent knows the moral reason behind most instructions we give.

_5_ Inappropriate, trendy fashions are not a source of conflict between us and our preadolescent.

_3_ Our preadolescent is characterized by coming to us in humility if he or she thinks our instructions are unfair.

_5_ Our preadolescent considers his or her siblings a part of his or her inner circle of best friends.

___4___ Our preadolescent doesn't get angry when things don't
go his or her way.

*Name of child:*_____ *Score:*_____ *Date:*_____

*Name of child:*_____ *Score:*_____ *Date:*_____

Scoring

145–165   Healthy; right on track; may need to fine-tune
some issues.

115–144   Healthy; basically on track; working on some
issues.

83–114   There are a number of behavioral concerns that, if
not corrected now, could lead to struggles and
conflict during adolescence.

66–82   There are many negative patterns signaling that
course correction is needed immediately.

33–65   Off course.

How did you do? By identifying your child's character strengths
and weaknesses now, you have gained a great advantage in parenting. And when you understand the information we are about to
give you, you can begin working objectively toward encouraging
and reinforcing the positive aspects of your child's character while
shoring up the weak ones.

But even with this advantage, please understand that neither
your child nor you will ever be perfect. Nor will your child's teen
years be bump-free—even if you maxed out on this test. Regardless

of how many books you read, seminars you attend, or tests you take, you're not going to do it right all the time. No one can. And that's okay as long as you're doing it right most of the time.

MARKS OF A HEALTHY FAMILY

Before we get into specific how-to's of middle-years parenting, consider the following characteristics drawn from over fifty households recognized by their communities as healthy families with teenagers.

From this sampling and from what we know about healthy families, we firmly conclude that healthy family relationships are cultivated, not inherited. This is a key concept to understand because it means the characteristics of a healthy family are within your grasp. With the right information and support, yours can be one of those families. And now we're going to share with you the fundamental principles that make it possible.

Let's begin by taking a look at seven positive characteristics of healthy families. You'll recognize them from questions on the test. If these traits aren't true of your family, don't panic. You can get there. In fact, you should expect to get there before your child becomes a teen.

Here are what healthy families with teenagers say are true of them.

1. Healthy families share core values that all members embrace and submit to.

Can a family live peaceably if individual members disagree on the meaning and importance of honesty, kindness, generosity, truthfulness, respect, honor, obedience, fairness, or friendship? Certainly not. Anarchy and endless infighting naturally follow when everyone does what is right in his or her own eyes. Try to nurture common values in all family members.

2. Healthy families recognize that maintaining the marriage is a priority for family health.

Most clinicians still believe that healthy marriages make for healthy families. Every child longs for the security that a healthy marriage brings to the family. The desire to know that Mom and Dad love each other does not diminish over time.

3. Healthy families know how to communicate with each other.

Good communication is not just about transmitting facts or giving commands such as "Take the garbage out now." It is the means by which we bond on a daily basis. It involves a willingness to be a listener as well as a talker. Families that don't talk together very often don't stay together.

4. In healthy families, parents are not afraid to say, "I was wrong."

As parents of a middle-years child, please understand that when you make a mistake, it's not only acceptable but important that you admit it. "Honey, I was wrong. Will you forgive me?"

5. Healthy families choose conflict resolution over conflict avoidance.

Healthy families choose to resolve conflict rather than run from it. Strong family relationships require mutual respect and the freedom for members to go to one another to deal with interpersonal issues. When we avoid conflict or situations that put us at odds with people we love and want to be loved by, we do so out of a fear of not being loved, appreciated, or understood. But running from a problem, or attempting to avoid it, breeds frustration, resentment, and bitterness. We strengthen our relationships not by avoiding conflicts, but by being willing to lovingly resolve them.

6. *Healthy families make time to be with each other and to attend one another's events.*

Cultivate a sense of family identity. Give each other time. It has been well said that a child spells *love* T-I-M-E. Once your child becomes a teenager, and particularly after he gets a driver's license, it will be even harder to find family times together. It won't happen on its own anymore.

You must set a precedent now. If you don't have time, make time. Healthy families carve out time to come together and recharge their relational batteries.

7. *Healthy families have a corporate sense of responsibility to all members.*

A corporate sense of responsibility is about more than just loyalty. Responsibility involves action: the choice to commit to the family unit and the decision to follow through on that commitment. This is characterized by a visible demonstration of responsible behavior. In response to a need, everyone pitches in and helps.

Families who share these characteristics are rare. But when you see one, you want what they have. That's not to say that healthy families are without problems. Stress, trials, conflicts, financial problems, and selfish attitudes confront healthy families as often as they do unhealthy ones. The difference is this: Healthy families know how to deal with stress; they know how to draw on one another's strengths to get through their trials; they know how to resolve conflict instead of avoiding it; they know how to confess their faults to one another.

These are things you can have in your family, too.

WARNING FLAGS

Now let's look at some traits that, if they are present in your middle-years child, may be cause for concern. If you see them in your child, they tell you that it is time for increased attention to his or her moral development.

1. Our child acts out when not in our presence or when in the presence of others who know and represent our family values.

There is no such thing as absolute moral consistency in adults, let alone children. There is always a degree of discrepancy between one's personal moral code and his or her behavior. But if your middle-years child ever becomes characterized by not caring who sees him doing something wrong, especially people who are familiar with your family's values, then the child's problem is one of shame—that is, the lack of it.

Shame is not the same thing as embarrassment. A woman who notices a run in her pantyhose during an interview may feel embarrassed. But there is nothing morally right or wrong about her situation. Shame, on the other hand, is a mechanism of the conscience. It acts to protect society when personal moral conviction is not sufficient to restrain wrongful behavior.

A friend of Gary has an abbreviation of his company name,

Bob's Lighting, on his license plate: BOBLITES. He is fairly well known around town, so people often recognize his pickup. In a casual conversation, Gary asked Bob if that license plate held him more accountable to obey the speed limit.

"Yes, it does," he admitted. "At times I tend to drive faster than the law permits. But now that I have my vanity license plate on my car, I think, 'What if people see me?' I would be ashamed if they thought of me as a traffic violator."

Bob's desire to do wrong (speeding) is restrained not by the love of virtue, but by the fear of shame associated with being caught by the public. Bob is not alone. We are all aware of the limits of behavior beyond which lies shame. There are certain social behaviors we avoid from fear of public judgment.

The moral makeup of our society complicates the problem. Today, our society is ruled by moral relativism, which means that the application of virtues and values are relative to each person's personal preference. Thus the application of values is neither constant nor consistent. That being the case, shame, which is dependent on a moral consensus of the populace, has no objective frame of reference. If all people can assign their own value to right and wrong, shame has no power. Without a consistent standard of right and wrong, no behavior is shameful.

A generation ago, we may have done things as children beyond what our parents would approve of, but shame usually restrained us from doing wrong in front of adults who knew us and our parents. We were conscious of bringing shame to our parents and family. Today, the voice of shame is often drowned out. To be sure your child hears that voice, you must hold her accountable for her actions. Rescuing a child from consequences teaches her only that there are none.

2. Our child tends to enjoy friends more than his or her own family; he or she is always asking to bring a friend along on family activities.

Children are social. They love companionship. At first, they merely want to do things with others. Those who satisfy this desire are their playmates. As they grow, children seek more than playmates—they seek friends. As they mature into pre- and early adolescence, their outside interests begin to expand, and their attachment to friends becomes deeper.

Should outside friendships supersede friendships inside the family? We say no. But we all know it does happen. If a child's family offers him little satisfactory companionship, he is deprived of the most important source of emotional security—his sense of belonging. When middle-years children fail to find relational satisfaction at home, they naturally turn to peers.

If your middle-years child displays a constant need for peer companionship, even during family times, take note. This is a warning sign that something is amiss in your family structure. Are you cultivating an interdependent family, or have you drifted toward an independent family in which the individual's desires come before those of the group? (More on interdependence and independence in chapter 9.)

Children accustomed to receiving comfort and approval from a few intimate and dependable relationships, such as those found in an interdependent family, tend to look to those same or similar relationships for comfort and companionship as they move through adolescence. If this is not the case with your child, extra effort toward interdependence in your family may be appropriate.

3. *The peers our child is attracted to come from families that do not share our values.*

Many years ago the Ezzos crossed the United States by car, heading for Los Angeles and camping along the way. They pulled into their last campsite at 6:30 P.M. on July 18, 1983. The KOA facility sat on a rise ten miles outside of Las Vegas overlooking the city.

It was nearly nightfall when the family finished pitching the tent. The business of setting up camp kept them occupied—so much so that they failed to notice the transformation of the city below. It was only after they sat down to rest that they noticed the alluring lights of Las Vegas. The family sat amazed, enchanted by the glittering scene. The Ezzos knew that Las Vegas represented a lifestyle foreign to them; nevertheless, they felt the urge to investigate its glamour.

What drives children to homes where the values are different from those of their parents? Three things: a child's natural attraction to that which is different; the bent of some children to move toward any prohibition; and a problem with family identity. The first two are neutral and normal. What we're concerned about is a possible problem with family identity that can lead to a child's misplaced allegiance.

Our identity is established by a set of socially understood reference points. The religious identity of a parish priest, for example, is revealed by his clothing, speech, and lifestyle. The rock musician is also recognized by his clothing, speech, and lifestyle. Their identities reveal their values. Both are identified by what they believe and how they act. People don't look at the rock musician and say, "Ah, there goes a religious man." Nor do they look at the priest and say, "Bet he plays a killer electric guitar."

Families have identities, too. We discuss family identity at length in chapter 9. For now, suffice it to say that if your middle-years child is drawn to a family with values different from yours, there may be problems with your family identity.

4. We are starting to hear similar negative reports about our child from a number of sources.

"No, my son isn't really lying," said Brian's mother. "He just likes to tell stories." This parent refused to acknowledge her son's lapse in morality, and so it was never dealt with.

Some children are very creative. At times, creative stories can be confused with lies. But if a number of people—schoolteachers, neighbors, people who watch your children on a regular basis—are coming to you with negative reports about your child, consider their words carefully.

The school administrator had not been the first one to approach Brian's parents about his dishonesty. Over time, many others had echoed a similar concern. Ever since his preschool days, Mom and Dad had dismissed Brian's predilection for the convenience of dishonesty. Only when the police started routinely knocking on the door did Brian's parents start to listen. By then it was too late. Their refusal to accept criticism of their son's behavior, let alone investigate, had helped shape him into a pathological liar.

It is embarrassing to hear negative reports about our children. We want to believe the best about them. It's also difficult to accept some things when we have not seen the evidence for ourselves. Our pride leads us to dismiss the possibility that what we are hearing is true. But if you are living and participating in a moral community, such a rebuke is often an expression of love.

Whether it's lying, disrespecting authority, or defacing property, what other people say may be true. Once again, it may be time to take the hard path and deal with the behavior. Holding a child accountable for his actions is your job as a parent. It is part of the process of instilling a moral conscience in him.

5. Although it is often done in a playful way, our child is continually seeking attention from the opposite sex.

This is a warning sign to Dad, in particular. We believe it is an indication that there is not enough physical expression of affection in your family.

In the course of our travels, we visit many families. In some homes we find children who are starved for physical affection. It's not that the parents are purposely neglectful, but that other urgent demands dominate their lives. As a result, their children's need to be touched goes unmet. Sometimes we are not in a home more than five minutes before children hop into our laps, seeking to be cuddled. Silently they are telling us, "Would you hold me? My Dad is too busy." Many little boys and girls have all the material advantages of life, yet lack what they really need—routine embraces.

As your child approaches the teen years, he or she will demonstrate a growing interest in the opposite sex. This is natural. Some flirting is to be expected. But is your child seeking affection from others? If so, this red flag is an indication that there is a need for

more physical touch at home, especially from Dac
role in chapter 12.)

6. *Our child, upon receiving the answer no from one parent, will go
ask the same question of the second parent without saying that the first
has already said no.*

Do you remember doing this when you were a kid? We probably
all tried it once or twice. Here, though, we are not talking about the
child who does so occasionally, but the child who is characterized
by seeking permission this way. This is a form of lying, since perti-
nent facts—such as "Mom already said no"—are omitted. This
behavior is a warning that your child has been trained to the *letter*
of the law, but not sufficiently to the *principle* of the rule.

In this case there is an external legal restriction at work instead
of an internal morality. To the child's way of thinking, the end (gain-
ing parental approval) justifies the means (the trickery that helped
secure the approval). This is a warning flag. If your child is characterized by such behavior, he or she has not yet internalized principles of right behavior. There will be more on this in Section II.

7. *Our child always bucks the system and wants to do things his own
way.*

Your children are not your equals. When it comes to wisdom, life
experience, and moral reasoning—not to mention age—you are
their superiors. They still need your guidance, whether they think
so or not. We gave this matter an entire chapter in *Childwise*, but it
is worth repeating here.

The middle-years child who always thinks he knows better

than his parents is waving a warning flag. The child who constantly tells you she's going to do such-and-such—instead of asking you for permission—is assuming a decision-making freedom for which she may not be ready. If your five-year-old believes she has the freedom to come and go at will at home, then what will stop her from wandering off at the mall or playground? It is not just the wandering off that is our concern, but the child's wholesale rejection of parental guidance at such a tender age.

When children enter the middle years, they carry forward childhood patterns of thinking. If they're experiencing frustration with your leadership at five, think what they might be like at age ten or fifteen if no course correction takes place in the middle years. Happily, course correction in this area is easy.

If your child is prone to be too independent, teach her to make this one minor adjustment in her communication. Instead of letting her tell you what she is going to do, instruct her to ask you for permission. Instead of saying "Dad, I'm going to…," she should say, "Dad, *may* I go to…?"

Words represent concepts. How we speak to our children—or allow our children to speak to us—instills in them patterns of right and wrong thinking, which ultimately directs their behavior. You simply cannot be an effective leader if your child is doing the leading. The "May I go?" reminds your middle-years child that he is still under Mom and Dad's tutelage.

Middle-years children need more from their parents than agreement; they need the security that parental authority brings into their world. Seeking permission helps shape a child's thinking regarding where he is along the road to independence.

8. Our child abuses verbal privileges. *Ben*

The child who has a sharp tongue, or who is bossy with —
even with you, is a child heading for trouble. Listen to the way your
middle-years child speaks to you. Is he demanding in his speech?
Does he tell you what to do? Does he seem to perceive you as his
equal—or worse, his inferior—rather than as the one who can give
him the loving guidance he so desperately needs?

This is related to the previous point. How we speak to our children and how we allow them to speak to us greatly affect their patterns of behavior. This interplay defines the boundaries of a child's
perception of self, self-reliance, and self-governance.

A child who abuses verbal freedoms may state facts, but his tone
will be offensive. When Mom says, "Honey, don't leave your socks
under the couch, please. Pick them up and put them in the laundry,"
the child responds, sassily, with a fact: "But Mom, Dad doesn't pick
up his socks. Why should I pick up mine?" While your son's statement might be technically accurate, and while Dad's example is not
the best, the tone in which your child speaks to you is troubling.

When parents leave such a tone unchallenged, it gives the child
a false self-sufficiency that will eventually misguide him in life. Here
is the problem: A child's sharp tongue does more than bring shame;
it severs relationships and in many cases prevents them. Teach your
middle-years child that he has the freedom to express his opinion,
but that he does not have the freedom to do so rudely.

If your middle-years child is talking back to you, and especially
if he is telling you what to do, it is a serious warning flag. It may be
time for you to retake the lead in this area and scale back the verbal
independence you have prematurely granted.

SUMMARY

One thing about having a beautician in the family: You get free haircuts. Years ago, haircut day for Gary required only a trip across the street to Anne Marie's sister's house. There, he would climb into a barber's chair, get draped, and let the hair trimming begin. Gary has never forgotten those long beautician scissors that snipped their way through his hair. Neither will he forget how Susan periodically paused, gently tapped his chin with the point of those scissors, and reminded him, "Chin up."

Self-evaluations are not always encouraging. If this chapter has left you with your head down, let us give you some words of encouragement: You are the parents of wonderful children—children who are moldable and who have an intrinsic desire to have a right relationship with you. Don't get in the pits by looking at a snapshot of where you are right now. Consider where you're going and what you can become as a family. Get your heads up. Get a fresh new perspective on your family. Chin up.

Chances are, you've noticed several characteristics of a healthy family right in your own home. They should encourage you. You may even have ideas for ways to enhance them. That's wonderful!

You also may have recognized a few of the warning flags, either in your own child or in someone you know. Don't be discouraged, even if every one of them is waving in your home.

This chapter is designed to give you a reference point, not to condemn you. Many public schools give a test at the beginning of the year, then give the same test at the end. The idea is to show how much the children have improved. Let this chapter serve as the pretest that will show off the improvement you will see in your family after you've learned and implemented the principles in this book.

The following chapters will give practical ideas about how to raise morally mature middle-years children. Some of the marks of a healthy family and the warning flags we've discussed in this chapter will be covered directly; others will not be. But the principles we introduce, if implemented in your family, will help you significantly raise your score on this survey.

BRINGING IT HOME

Take some time now to discuss this chapter with your spouse. Talk about how you scored on the test and what you think you could do better, even now. Then ask each other this question: Where do we want to be in a few years? Through discussion, begin to build a shared vision for what your family relationships will look like in the future. It's amazing how helpful it is to have a plan.

Chapter Three

Leading by Influence

*T*he greatest transition of middle-years parenting rests more on the shoulders of Mom and Dad than on Junior. How should you use your authority during these years? More appropriately, how can you learn to use less of it?

No parenting topic causes greater confusion than the administration of parental authority in child training. Parents and experts alike are polarized over this issue. But they shouldn't be. Let us assure you: Parental authority is not a bad thing. Quite the contrary. It is absolutely necessary in order to maintain the balance among personal freedom, responsibility, and obligation.

Parental authority represents the right of parents to insist upon conformity and compliance, especially in these three vital areas of life: morality, health and safety, and life skills.

First, parental authority is necessary to officiate a child's morality. By your authority you lead, guide, encourage, correct, and right the wrongs perpetrated by and on your child. By your moral authority you bring about right moral outcomes.

If your child is rude or discourteous, you work to correct it. If your child selfishly takes a toy from another, you fix the moral transgression. You return the toy to the offended party, and you teach the offender the ethics of private ownership, sharing, and how to ask for a toy. You also teach in such times the virtues of grace, mercy, forgiveness, and restoration.

You also exercise persuasive authority with regard to health and safety issues. You insist that your child take his terrible-tasting medicine, keep his seat belt buckled, brush his teeth, chew his vitamins, and take his bath. You call him away from the busy street and the river's edge. In each case, you insist on compliance.

When it comes to life skills, you insist that the cereal bowl be placed in the sink and not left on the table. You enforce a full half hour of piano practice every day. With your authority, backed by your resolve, you insist that the bike be placed in the garage, the homework be done on time, and the dirty clothes be placed in the hamper.

Can parental authority be abused? Certainly! And at times it has been. Too much authority leads to totalitarianism. Insufficient authority leads to social chaos. This is just as true for families as it is for nations.

The overly permissive parent looks at the overly authoritarian parent and says: "I don't want to be like *that* mother and father. They're too strict!" Meanwhile, the authoritarian parent looks at the permissive household and says, "I don't want my children acting like *that*. Those kids are out of control!"

The permissive parent who controls too little and the authoritarian parent who controls too much both deprive their children of basic skills necessary for healthy adolescence. Too often these kids hit the teen years either underdirected or undermotivated.

You do have another choice. You probably don't need to increase your control at this stage of the game, nor are you likely to need to back away from your authority. As you approach your child's teen years, you can transition from relying on the power of your authority to tapping into the power of your relational influence. This is the one great middle-years transition every parent must make.

LESS IS MORE

Now that your child is in the middle years, it's time to ask yourself: Am I using more, or less of my authority to bring about moral conformity? Consider carefully your answer to this question. While many parents feel tempted to exert greater control during the middle and teen years, we want to stress that you must begin to rely less upon the power of authority. As your preteen approaches adolescence, the need for your parental rule should decline in direct proportion to his increased rate of moral self-rule.

The middle years are a potentially confusing time not just for your child, but also for you as a parent. You know your child is changing, but you can't pin down precisely how or what exactly lies behind it. You may fear the unknown and be anxious about what lies ahead. This apprehension often sparks the desire to increase your control. At times you may feel that the best way to manage the future is to constrict boundaries to more fully control your preteen. The child makes one wrong move and sparks ignite. The child's entire sense of freedom is left in the ashes, and everyone's scarred emotionally.

Or perhaps you go to the other extreme and completely surrender, saying: "What am I to do? My teenager is going to do whatever he wants anyway." As the teen years draw near, you find yourself pulled into the despair felt by so many parents in our society. You throw up your hands, shake your head, and go about the business of living your own life amidst the chaos created by a child beyond control.

FROM "YOU WILL" TO "WILL YOU?"

During the middle years, you should be moving away from leadership by parental decree and toward leadership by life principle. The "because Mommy said so" style simply won't be as effective for an older child who is capable of understanding the reasons behind your decisions.

It should be your goal to come to the place where you can lead your child only through your influence. Say this: "By the time my child reaches adolescence, I will have exchanged rule-centered leadership for principle-centered leadership."

THE AUTHORITY EXCHANGE

Mankind has always struggled with authority. Yet it is absolutely essential. Law and order for the family and society depend on its proper administration. Authority, properly administered, guides by both encouragement and restraint. As your child matures, your leadership style will also change as you begin to rely less on authority and more on influence.

As you go through these middle years, the training phase, you need to learn how to prepare to be a sideline coach. Remember, you're installing everything in your child you can so they can make more and more moral decisions independently. It is your task during these years to transition away from authoritarian teacher to encouraging coach. The exchange must be complete—not in the process—by the time the teen years begin. Here's how Carla, a young mother of three, began that transition with her ten-year-old daughter.

At the end of one of the Ezzos's parenting classes, Carla approached Anne Marie with a question. She listened attentively to Anne Marie's response, reluctantly agreed to try what she had suggested, and went home. When she returned to class the next week, she shared the following results before an audience of her peers.

"I have three girls. Whitney is ten, Brenda is eight, and Carissa is four. Like most parents, I have a real fear about this next phase of parenting, especially with my ten-year-old. I had a little talk with Anne Marie last week about an incident involving Whitney and sharing.

"I explained to Anne Marie that Whitney had a bag of popcorn and that Brenda asked for some. Whitney said no. This really bothered me because my eight-year-old is so generous with her sister, almost to a fault. So I intervened and told Whitney that she had to share. She finally did.

"When I thought through the incident I knew I hadn't done the right thing, but I didn't know what I'd done wrong. So I asked Anne Marie what she thought I should do. I was surprised when she told me to think about not always intervening with my authority and forcing my kids to share with each other. This was a frightening prospect for me. Asking me to give up my control? I said to Anne Marie, 'How long will I be doing this? What if this goes on forever?' Anne Marie assured me it would not, but asked that I try it for several weeks to see what happened.

"The next day another incident took place. Whitney had some mints and Brenda asked for some. Whitney said no, and Brenda immediately looked to me for help. I told Brenda, 'If Whitney doesn't want to share with you, that's fine. Sharing must come from our hearts or it is not real sharing.' Brenda protested for a few moments, and I went about my business.

"A little later my ten-year-old came to me. 'It's okay if I don't share, Mom?" she asked. "Is that what you said?' I replied, 'Yes, that's what I said.' Whitney left, but at that very moment I could see something had changed in her heart. Five minutes later she was generously sharing her mints with Brenda.

"The next day, all I heard from the two girls was: 'Can I borrow your this?' 'Can I play with your that?' I was shocked. Noncoercive sharing was foreign to my children. It was foreign to me. Yet there they were doing it.

"I called my ten-year-old aside and asked, 'Whitney, why are you so willing to share all of a sudden?' 'Mom,' she said, 'this is how I always felt, but you never let me do it without telling me I had to. I wanted to show you how I felt, but you never let me do it without making me. I wanted to show you that I know how to make a wise decision and do the things you and Daddy taught us.'

"I went home last week and gave up trying to control all the outcomes by using my authority. In a very marginal way, I started to use the power of my influence by speaking truth in love with my kids. I can tell you that in one week's time, Whitney has become a different child—mostly because she has a different mom. And while I am still using my authority with Brenda, I can see why I need less and less of it to guide Whitney.

"There is one more thing I learned through this experience. In the past, when I tried to control all outcomes, I was actually robbing my kids of the joy of doing right. I can see that now. At Whitney's age, there is no joy in doing right when the actions required are always tied to my authority."

Can you relate to Carla's story? Please note, this mother did not abandon her authority. She simply began phasing out her "because Mom said" kind of authority with her eldest child. Now she works to bring about right outcomes by leading through her influence.

Consider for a moment how you once controlled everything about your child's day. When your child was five, you no longer controlled or directed his day to the same extent as you did when he was an infant. At five, he could come and go from the backyard, pick out his own board games, play with his hamster, or go to his room and play with a puzzle. Because he continually demonstrated responsible behavior, parental policing was no longer necessary in these areas. Although parental authority is still a considerable influence in a five-year-old's life, it is not as sweeping in its control as it was a few years earlier.

The same holds true of a ten-year-old. With the increase of self-rule there is a direct decrease in the amount of parental policing required. Gradually, parental control is replaced by parental influence. Moral maturity emancipates the child, allowing him to direct his own behavior in harmony with family values.

Consider twelve-year-old Alyssa, who needed a new swimsuit. Modesty was a major issue for Mom. Alyssa, however, seemed bent on a scanty two-piece version she had spotted in her favorite teen magazine. The battle lines were drawn. Or were they? Certainly, Mom could have held her ground, selected the suit she approved of, and marched on to the next altercation. She might have won the battle, but not the war. For this mom, the conflict would have ended in a stalemate, and yet another trek around the mall would lay ahead.

Next time, Alyssa's Mom might try leading by relational influence. Mom could make a suggestion and support it by the reason for her preference and the moral implications of the choice. Then she could give Alyssa time alone to scout out her options. Most likely, when provided the opportunity to respond responsibly on her own, Alyssa will make a selection with which everyone can live. If not, the suit can always be returned, and Alyssa might temporarily lose the privilege of making an independent purchase.

SUMMARY

Certainly we are not suggesting you eliminate house or family rules. Your middle-years child (and later, your teen) is still accountable to you. There are community tasks and responsibilities that need to be maintained. Your child still needs to take out the trash, make his own bed, clean up after himself, be home at a reasonable hour, and, yes, comply with parental instruction. However, the basic tasks of life should take on new meaning—a moral one in response to a relationship to the family. No longer are they simply responses to an impersonal set of rules reinforced by coercive authority.

Like both moms in the examples, you may feel a bit awkward as you begin the transition from authority to influence. However, this change is absolutely necessary. Understand that you will use far more of your authority with your eight-year-old than you will with your twelve-year-old. But by the end of the middle years, the authority exchange should be complete.

BRINGING IT HOME

1. What does parental authority represent?

2. Upon what basis should parental rule decline during the middle years?

3. What are the four phases of parenting?

4. In Carla's story, what was she afraid of giving up?

5. Where are you right now in the process of authority exchange?

Chapter Four

Raising a Responsible Middle-Years Child

"My, what an obedient child."

When was the last time you heard that compliment about a member of your brood? There is no question that obedient children are a joy to be with, teach, and lead. Ask any public school teacher wrestling daily with a number of disobedient children. There is just something about the public display of obedience that attracts not only the applause of a grateful society, but the internal applause of a parent's own heart. Such a compliment means others have noticed your commitment to instilling virtue in your child.

Be warned, though: The "My, what an obedient child" compliment comes with an expiration date. While it might be flattering praise for your preschooler, it is not a compliment to your preteen.

Here is another middle-years transition you desire for your child: from obedience to responsibility.

MAKING THE TRANSFER

When your parenting is over, which would you rather have raised: an obedient child or a responsible child? There is a difference. Though obedience is very important in early child training, it is only a stepping-stone to a greater goal—yes, even a greater virtue. Obedience versus responsibility—what is the difference? Obedience is required conformity. Responsibility is voluntary conformity. Obedience is submission to a person. Responsibility is submission to a principle.

A child who does right on his own volition (instead of because he is reminded to) will be far better equipped for life than one who is dependent upon someone telling him what to do.

How are you doing in this area of parenting with your middle-years child? Are you working to raise a responsible child, or are you still making obedience the big issue?

WHAT DOES IT LOOK LIKE?

It's called follow-through, completion, stick-to-itiveness, perseverance, finishing the task at hand, and taking full ownership. Ultimately, this is how we want our children to be characterized. When a task is given them, they know how to complete it without prompting, bribing, threatening, or a continual barrage of reminders. Unfortunately, sometimes parents are their own worst enemy when it comes to equipping their children with these virtues.

Every night, ten-year-old Ben takes his shower right on time. He emerges from the bathroom with tousled hair, his bathrobe snuggled around him, and walks to his room to dress. Such a fine young lad!

But here's where this recurring situation turns ugly. Mom enters the steamy bathroom and finds, not to her surprise, dirty socks and jeans draped over the toilet, soapsuds flowing out of the tub, puddles in every corner, and in the middle of it all, one hunter green bath towel lying on the floor, a monument to Ben's magnificent achievement.

As is her custom, Mom goes ballistic. She grumbles the whole time she wipes up the water-soaked floor, mumbling, "How many times must I remind this boy?" Didn't I remind him yesterday to use the hamper? What part of using a shower curtain doesn't he understand? Why can't he get it right? She considers sitting him down to explain it—again.

Mom yearns to turn this situation around. But how? Until Mom and Dad learn how to transfer ownership responsibility for follow-through behavior to Ben, he has no reason to become accountable for his actions. No child will develop responsible initiative as long as Mom and Dad are always prompting, reminding, or nagging.

The goal of this chapter is to teach you how to pass to your child a sense of behavioral ownership and how to implant a self-generated sense of responsibility. You want your child to be characterized by diligence in following through with his actions, mistakes, messes, and misdeeds. But how do you get your middle-years child there?

You will know you have arrived when you are no longer the

catalyst for your child's initiative. Constantly reminding him what is right, wrong, or expected not only frustrates the parents, but also robs the child of any motivation to follow through for himself. From the child's perspective, why take ownership of today's lesson if he's going to be schooled in it again tomorrow?

Instilling a stick-to-itive virtue in your children is not as difficult as it might appear. There are two social realities that cannot be ignored in the process.

Reality One: Parents own all behaviors until the child is both intellectually ready and physically capable to take ownership.

This principle acknowledges that parents are responsible for their young child's messes, mistakes, and misdeeds. If your two-year-old spills pancake syrup on the family pet, you do not assign him the task of giving the dog a bath. If your four-year-old accidentally spills the open can of paint on the garage floor, you don't sit back and let her clean up the mess. She will only make a bigger mess.

So what happens? You step in. In these cases, the child's mess is your mess. His mistakes and accidents belong to you. You're responsible because the child is not old enough to be responsible for rectifying the problems her actions created. But if your ten-year-old makes the mess, hopefully she can be trusted to take a major role in the cleanup effort.

Reality Two: In child training, all behavior belongs to parents until they transfer ownership to the child.

The question parents must wrestle with is which behaviors belong to them and which belong to their child. In the examples above,

Mom and Dad own the outcomes of the spilled paint because of the age of the children involved. But as children grow, their capacity to assume responsibility and take ownership also grows. While a two-year-old could not give the dog a bath, an eight-year-old could.

So how do you know when to make behavioral ownership transfers? To answer that question, we need to consider the two phases of accountability training: *preaccountability* and *accountability*. These phases reflect the two realities mentioned above.

PREACCOUNTABILITY AND ACCOUNTABILITY TRAINING

The preaccountability phase is the period of training in which the child is in the process of learning specific skills, courtesies, and patterns of right behavior. During this phase, the child is not held fully responsible for his own actions. Remember the spilled paint? A four-year-old cannot be held accountable for cleanup. She's too young, inexperienced, and lacks the skills for such a task. In this area of life she lives in a preaccountable world. Mom and Dad must assume responsibility for her actions. Much of this is experienced during the first six years of your child's life, when Mom and Dad's direct leadership makes up much of his day.

For example, there was a time when Mom used to put out the paint set and coloring book for three-year-old Lucy. Afterwards, Mom cleaned up the mess because Lucy wasn't ready for that task. This occurred in the preaccountability phase. But the day came when Mom began to show Lucy how she could get her paint set down from the shelf, lay out the newspaper on the kitchen table, and then, after paint time, clean up after herself. This is making the transition to the accountability phase.

Mom was teaching responsible behavior for a specific task. As Lucy grew and became more responsible, she learned to take more and more ownership of her own behavior. Eventually, Lucy—not Mom—was held accountable for her own paint-time activities. Mom had properly transferred accountability to Lucy.

Your child will learn new behaviors and courtesies throughout childhood and preadolescence. Therefore this process—preaccountability training, followed by accountability training—will be repeated throughout your child's development. It starts with the introduction of a behavioral expectation, allows time for assimilation of the new behavior, and then transitions to the child accepting ownership of the behavior. The preaccountability phase might last months for some tasks and some children, minutes for others. But once your child reaches the accountability phase of training, he owns the behavior. Don't take the ownership back.

MONKEYS ON YOUR BACK

"Brian put your bike away. Brian, did you hear me? I'm not going to tell you again. I mean it! Put it away. Now, Brain! Don't make me call your father."

Who's got the problem here? Not Brian. Brian's mom is a threatening-repeating mother. The habit of repeating instructions, redrawing lines in the sand, and spewing out empty threats in hopes that the child will comply is one of the most ineffective modes of parenting.

There is another, subtler form of this futile parenting style. What happens when the reminders aren't repeated in successive sentences but over a period of hours, days, or weeks? If you have to remind your child every day to put his schoolbag away, feed the dog, make his bed, hang up the towel, or any other assigned responsibility, you are acting just like Brian's mom. The difference is only in the frequency of your threatening and repeating. The form is different, but the substance is the same.

No wonder the child doesn't appropriate your instructions: There are no consequences for neglecting them, and they'll be repeated tomorrow anyway, so why remember them today? At what point will you stop reminding? Constantly reminding a child to do what is expected only means you have no expectation.

When parents continue to instruct and remind their children how to behave after accountability training has been achieved, they are taking back ownership of a behavior that should no longer belong to them. When parents do this, they pick up unwelcome behavioral "monkeys."

Monkeys are a great analogy for what is happening here. Monkeys can be cute little critters, but they can also be bothersome pests, especially when they start to climb all over you and weary you with their weight and busyness. We use the monkey analogy because monkeys love jumping. In parenting, there are behavioral monkeys that belong to your children. The problem is that monkeys love jumping, and they love jumping back on you. That's the wrong direction. Your goal is to get rid of the monkeys, not collect them. Here are three principles to consider.

1. In the early years, parents carry all the monkeys.

Parents carry all behavioral monkeys until the child is old enough to carry them. This is true of life skills, matters of health and safety, and certainly morality. There comes a day when your child is ready to take ownership of his own actions, behaviors, attitudes, and obligations.

Remember Ben and the bathroom mess? Responsibility for follow-through was his. But it wasn't always so. There was a period of preaccountability, when he was learning to become responsible with the freedom of taking his own shower. Mom and Dad owned the responsibility for cleanup. But once Ben understood what was required of him and was capable of following through, the ownership monkey passed to him. At least it should have.

2. Once the monkey has passed to the child, it must stay with the child.

There are certain behavioral expectations that you passed to your child a long time ago: knowing how to clean her room, pick up after herself, extend a courtesy, or feed the cat. Those monkeys belong to your child.

The problem is that these monkeys love to jump back to their original carriers—Mom and Dad. They love it when Mom or Dad start feeding and caring for them. And your children love it when you do, too. But those monkeys do not belong to you. They belong to your son or daughter.

3. Given a chance, behavioral monkeys will try to jump back to the parent.

When do behavioral monkeys jump from the child back to the parent? When a parent continues to assume ownership of a behavior that rightly belongs to the child. Parents do this by constantly reminding a child what to do after the child has reached the accountability phase of training.

You know you have too many monkeys when you become increasingly frustrated and annoyed at the child's lack of initiative in assuming responsibility for his behavior. Multiply the number of monkeys by the number of children you have.

Darece's Story

"I'm tired of always reminding them!" Have your ever whispered that phrase—or shouted it? When Darece first heard about the monkey concept, she immediately thought of breakfast time.

"My five children all have little chores to do before they sit down for breakfast, but I found myself asking them every morning, 'Did you make your bed?' 'Did you put your books in your school-bag?' 'Nicholas, did you feed the dog?' With five kids, there is bound to be a 'No, not yet, Mom' in there somewhere. These are smart kids. Why do I always have to remind them?"

Darece resolved the problem in a big way. She sat the kids down and announced that she no longer was going to remind them of what was expected. Instead, they simply would not have the *freedom* to sit down for breakfast if they did not first take care of their morning responsibilities. In fact, this is the great monkey repellent phrase: "Do you have the freedom to…?"

The next morning, ten-year-old Nicholas came out of his room and headed for the breakfast table. He stopped in his tracks, looked at Mom, then at the breakfast table. With a smile he said, "I don't think I have the freedom to be here right now. I'll be right back, Mom." Off Nicholas went to take care of a forgotten chore.

What a relief for Darece. For months she had repeated herself every morning. By always asking her children if their chores were done, beds made, school lunches ready, and papers signed, she was collecting all their monkeys. In doing so, she had taken back ownership responsibilities that belonged to the kids. By 8:00 A.M., with five children in the house, Mom had picked up a dozen monkeys. And the day had just begun.

As long as Mom is there to remind them what to do, the kids never have to be concerned about doing anything on their own. In the child's view of things, it is easy to see what is going on. If Nicholas gets to the table and Mom is too busy to ask about his chores, he wins. The worst thing that could happen would be hearing Mom's reminder and having to go back and do what was expected.

All this can be solved by the simple little phrase: "Do you have the freedom to…?"

MONKEY REPELLENT

It is helpful to think of privileges in terms of freedoms that children can earn or lose. For example, your eight-year-old has been playing in his room all morning and decides he now wants to play outside. He heads for the slides, but Mom intercepts him. "Where are you going, Danny?"

"Outside to play."

The next questions that seem to flow from the lips of most moms go like this: "Did you pick up your toys? How about your puzzle; is that put away? And all of your little army men; are they put back in the box?"

With her checklist of questions, the responsibility for a clean room just jumped back on Mom's shoulders. If Danny's Mom is going to keep reminding him of what he should have done, then he never has to take the initiative to do it in the first place. Like Nicholas, what could Danny lose? If he gets caught, the worst that will happen is that he will have to listen to Mom's lecture about responsibility and march back to his room. Danny knows there is a good chance that Mom won't ask at all—so much the better, to his way of thinking.

There is a better way to handle this. Instead of a checklist of questions, try some monkey repellent: "Danny, I know you where just playing in your room. Do you have the freedom to play outside right now?" With that question, the burden (monkey) of responsibility for a clean room stays where it belongs—on Danny. Instead of Mom telling him what needs to be done, Danny takes ownership of what needs to be done.

Eventually, Danny will learn that when he wants to leave one activity and go to another, Mom is going to ask the big "do you have the freedom?" question. Just knowing that question is coming will serve as a wonderful catalyst to motivate almost any child to accept responsibility for the here and now.

Most children really do want to look you in the eye and honestly say, "Yes, Mom, I do have the freedom to play outside. My room is picked up; my homework is finished; and my chores are done."

If a child tells his parents that he has the freedom to do something when he really doesn't, consequences are necessary. If Danny had lied and said his toys were picked up, of course he would need to go pick them up. But that is not the consequence, since he was responsible to do that in the first place. After he picks up his toys, the consequence is imposed: He loses the freedom of going outside for a period of time to remind him to be honest the next time he is asked.

The phrase "Do you have the freedom to do that?" repels monkeys because it puts the burden of ownership back on the child. The child thinks, "What must I do before I have the freedom to do anything else?"

Contrast the expectations associated with the "do you have the freedom?" question with the daily checklist of parental reminders. Which one do you think will provoke a child to greater initiative and follow-through? With the first, you are teaching your child to be responsible. That's a long-term benefit. With the reminders, you are correcting only one instance of disobedience.

The simple question, "Danny, do you have the freedom?" forces him to think, *Well, do I?* He starts reviewing what Mom or Dad has just said. He looks around the room for things lying out or anything else that might trigger his memory. You'll be amazed at the things he comes up with that he needs to do first—things you weren't even aware of or had forgotten about. That's the sign of a bona fide conscience, and it's a beautiful thing to behold.

Eventually you want your question, "Danny do you have the freedom to…?" to become Danny's question, "Do I have the freedom to…? An additional benefit is that children who develop this pattern of thinking become less susceptible to peer pressure because they are not dependent on others to do their thinking for them.

THE PLEASE-AND-THANK-YOUS

Let's take this money business a little farther. There is a category of behavior we call the please-and-thank-yous of life. These are the moral courtesies you have attempted to instill in your child. Learning to say please, for example, when one wants something is a moral courtesy that every child should learn to extend.

Your eight-year-old child comes to you and says, "Mom, can I have a Coke?" Never mind for a moment that *may I* is always nicer than *can I*. Generally, the typical response of Mom would be something like, "What do you say?" or "What's the magic word?" or "How do you ask?" But by asking these questions, Mom takes the monkey from her child. She has excused him from owning the courtesy.

To avoid taking this monkey, Mom could respond, "No, I am sorry I do not have the freedom to give you a drink right now." Through this little exercise, the child *will* take ownership of her own behavior in the future. Remember, if Mom is always reminding, the child never has to learn the lesson.

Normally what happens in the scene above is this: The child instantly responds to Mom: "May I *please* have a Coke?" If this were a younger child, Mom might decide to go ahead and let the child have the drink. But for a middle-years child, you may decide that additional time might help the learning process. Here we offer a note of caution. Do not say, "Come back in five minutes and ask properly." While your son may suffer a temporary consequence from a five-minute delay, he is less likely to appreciate the lesson or self-generate responsibility. Most likely tomorrow's request will lack a "please."

Try this instead. "I'm sorry, I don't have the freedom to give you a coke right now. I'm going to ask you to sit down at the table for a few minutes to think about why that is so."

Giving children time to morally process right and wrong is absolutely necessary to help them take ownership of skills, and courtesies. In this case you are listening for more than "I can't have coke because I *didn't* say please." You're listening for much more.

REFLECTIVE SIT-TIME—TAKING OWNERSHIP OF ETHICAL ISSUES

Transferring ownership of responsible behavior goes far beyond chores, breakfast routines, and schoolbags. Ultimately, you want your children to take ownership of their moral actions. It is our experience that nothing can speed this process more than what we call *reflective sit-time*.

A reflective sit-time affords the child the opportunity to sit and think about what he should have done or said. It is a corrective strategy, not a punitive one. It is to help bring a child to repentance, forgiveness, and restoration, to help a child morally process and evaluate his or her circumstance; and to take ownership for present and future responses. Reflective sit-time is a great tool for children six years of age and older.

To demonstrate the power of reflective sit-times, we will offer some scenarios. The first demonstrates what happens when the parent wrongly assumes ownership of ethical issues. The second demonstrates what happens when the child is given an opportunity to own his or her attitudes and actions. All our examples are true-life stories.

Cindy's Story

"Mom," Cindy said, "will you sign my news report for school?"

"Let me review them," Mom said. "Cindy, what is this?"

"It's a paragraph I had to write for current events. Will you just sign it, please?"

"You are not turning this in, young lady," Mom said. "Cindy, you are eleven years old. Just look at it—this is sloppy work."

"Mom! It doesn't have to be perfect. The teachers don't care what it looks like." They just want today's headline news.

"Well, I care," Mom said. "Cindy, look at me when I'm talking to you. And don't roll your eyes at me, young lady."

"I wasn't rolling my eyes! Mom! You're being unfair."

"Cindy, don't talk to your mother that way. Child, you need an attitude adjustment."

"What are you going to do—send me to my room?"

"Yes, I think I will. Good idea. I am tired of reminding you about your work and the way you talk to me. It isn't right. You have no respect for me."

"What did I do?"

"What did you do young lady? I'll tell you what you did. You wrote a sloppy paper and argued with me. You rolled your eyes at me and talked back to me. That's what you did. What you need to do, young lady, is apologize to me for all these things and then redo your paper—neatly this time. Whether you believe me or not, the work you hand in at school represents me, too. Frankly, I don't want the teachers thinking I don't care if you do sloppy work. I don't know why I have to keep telling you these things over and over and over again. When will you ever learn?"

❖ ❖ ❖

What do you think? How would you have handled the situation?

Unfortunately, this scene reflects an all-too-common parenting style. Cindy's mom picked up her daughter's monkeys like a zookeeper. With Mom doing all the thinking and talking, Cindy really did not have to think at all. Mom was right there telling her. She did not have to morally process the rightness or wrongness of her actions. Mom did it for her. As long as that continues, Mom can expect Cindy's poor behavior to continue.

Later in this chapter we will discuss what could have been done differently. For now, let's work through our second scenario, this time using a *reflective sit-time*.

Whitney's Story

She did it again! Why couldn't she get this? George felt his frustration growing. Seven-year-old Whitney was always in too much of a hurry when she got out of the van. She had the bad habit of launching the van door aside and letting it crash on its back hinges. The din of metal on metal was George's reminder that his oft-repeated message, "Open the door carefully," hadn't sunk in yet.

Normally, George would give Whitney a lecture—unwittingly gathering up all of his daughter's monkeys. "Whitney, you know better. How many times do I have to tell you to slide that door back carefully? I'm tired of telling you. You're going to break the door. You've got to be more careful with Aunt Jenny's van. Do you understand?" With the lecture complete, Whitney would say, "Sorry, Dad" and be on her way.

But this time George tried a new tactic. Instead of telling

Whitney all she did wrong, he directed her to a chair in the living room. "Whitney, I want you to sit here and think about what just happened. I'll be back in a few minutes to check on you."

At first Whitney protested. "Dad, I don't know why you're making me sit."

"That's why I want you to think about it. And, Whitney, you can have nothing in your hands while you're thinking about this problem. Put the couch pillow down."

Ten minutes passed before George returned. He gently asked, "Can you tell Dad what you did wrong?"

"Yes," Whitney said contritely. "I wasn't careful with Aunt Jenny's van door."

"That's right," George said. "Now, Whitney, I want you to sit and think about this question: What must you do to make this right? I'll be back in a few minutes."

Whitney pondered the question. Here she faced the real test of her moral knowledge. The question was a test of George's parenting as well as Whitney's moral processing skills. Had her parents done enough work in training their daughter? Had they deposited sufficient knowledge in her moral warehouse?

In a few minutes, George returned to find Whitney's eyes cloudy and her heart heavy. She knew her wrong extended back further than just this one episode. George asked: "Whitney, do you know what you must do to make this right?"

"I think so," she said, tears brimming her eyes. "When Aunt Jenny comes back to town, I need to call her and ask for forgiveness for not being careful with her car."

George smiled. Whitney had finally gotten it. She had taken

moral ownership of her own wrong and the way to make it right. The best thing about it was that she had gotten there without Dad. When it happens like this, the lesson sticks—initiative is gained.

We are happy to provide an epilogue to Whitney's story. It has been several months now since this real-life episode took place. This little girl truly learned her lesson. Whitney now has a wonderful self-owned sensitivity about how to treat property belonging to others—especially how to exit a car with care.

In our example of Cindy and her current events report, Cindy never really took ownership of her behavior. Mom did it for her. Any positive impact on her behavior was temporary. Mom did not empower her child to take ownership of her mistakes. There was no time to morally process, so there was no moral internalization, no change of heart. Just another lecture.

Whitney's heart, in contrast, was transformed. She was challenged and her inner moral voice was stirred. Her conscience began to speak of right and wrong, carefulness and carelessness. George challenged his daughter to think and process morally, to take ownership. That is exactly what a reflective sit-time will do for your child.

Amy's Story

Briana was celebrating her eleventh birthday with her family. They were traveling on her birthday, but her parents had brought along many of her gifts. Her special present that year was something she had been wanting for a long time: a vanity for her bedroom. After opening her gifts, Briana's dad told her that she had another gift waiting for her at home. Briana's face lit up as she began to imagine what it might be. Then Amy, Briana's eight-year-old sister, blurted out, "I know what it is, Briana—it's your vanity!" Her surprise destroyed, Briana's tears began to flow.

Amy was instructed by her parents to go into another room to sit and think about what she had done and be prepared to give an answer. Amy was asked to morally process what had just happened. Her parents were expecting more from her than, "I told Briana what her gift was." They expected her to move to a much deeper level of contemplation.

After forty-five minutes, Amy tearfully confessed what she had done, and her confession was beautiful: "I stole Briana's joy of receiving the gift as a surprise." Wow! Where did that answer come from? From an ability to morally process. Here's an eight-year-old child coming up with an adult-sized answer.

The prerequisite to moral reasoning is knowing moral truth. This assumes that Mom and Dad have been actively implanting moral truth in Amy's heart. (We'll talk about moral maturity in Section II.) In Amy's case, they had. From the time when she was three and had wanted to pick flowers in the public park, they had told her the "why" of right and wrong. This deposit of moral truth created an infrastructure of logical thought that enabled Amy to process deeply. Without a knowledge of virtues and values, children will be limited in their ability to reason and process moral situations.

After hearing Amy's response, her parents instructed her to think about what she must do to make it right. She sat alone for an additional thirty minutes before she responded with another profound answer. She came to realize that she could never give Briana back her joy about this gift. What a lesson in life. Her parents agreed, reminding her that she must guard against taking things from others that she can never give back.

When presenting this concept in seminars, we are commonly asked who determines the length of the sit-time, the child or the parent? The answer depends on the context of the wrong and the child's age. With younger children, parents should monitor the child's readiness to share. In Whitney's case, George checked in after fifteen minutes to see how she was doing. But Amy's parents allowed her to choose the length. For some children, a reflective sit-time might take five minutes. For others, it might take much longer. Make these decisions based on the complexity of the situation and the age and moral readiness of your child.

 How You Know It Has Worked

A reflective sit-time has been effective when the answer the child gives comes from the level of the conscience. A satisfactory response has two components: *what I did* (what was wrong, how was it wrong, why it was wrong, who it hurt) and *what I can do to make it right*. If the child comes back with a shallow response, send him back for more time. The next step is to carry out the things he needs to do to make it right.

SUMMARY

Go back and review the conversation between Cindy and her Mom. Try to spot the places where Mom is taking monkeys back on herself. Now let's consider how she could have handled the situation differently.

"Mom," Cindy said, "will you sign my papers for school?"

"Why does your teacher want me to sign them?" Mom asked.

First, Mom needs to know the reason the teacher wants parents of her students to sign homework. Cindy is responsible to supply this information unless Mom has received it directly from the teacher through a note or personal contact. If by signing the paper Mom is indicating to the teacher that she thinks Cindy's work is acceptable, then Mom has assumed part of the responsibility for Cindy's schoolwork.

When working in tandem with a teacher, this is not necessarily wrong for parents to do. In any case, parents should be concerned about the work their children do. Certainly parents can be working with their children to teach them to be neat and orderly, and this would apply to how they do their chores, dress themselves, and complete their school assignments. All these things considered, just how can Cindy's mom help her accept responsibility for her actions and attitudes?

Mom looked at the paper, then put it down. "Cindy, I'm sorry, but I don't have the freedom to sign this work."

"But it's due today!"

"I understand that. You are certainly free to turn it in, but I cannot sign it."

"But the teacher won't accept it without your signature."

"Cindy, I understand that this puts you in a predicament. But the responsibility for getting your work done neatly and in on time is yours, not mine. Maybe you just need to take a minute and figure out what to do about it."

Cindy was well aware of when this assignment was due and how long she would need to complete it. It really didn't matter why the work was not neat. The point was, it was Cindy's obligation to take care of it. Ultimately, Cindy's mom was saying that she was willing for Cindy to receive a lower grade. If she shielded Cindy from the consequences of her actions, she was not doing her daughter any favors. And she was taking back a monkey, which didn't do herself any favors, either.

When parents refuse to take ownership of monkeys that rightly belong to their children, it eliminates power struggles. It equips children to think for themselves, to process moral truth in life's varied scenarios, and to take responsibility for their own behavior.

We sometimes wonder what our society would look like if everyone took responsibility for his or her behavior. How much nicer the shopping malls and airports of our world would be. How much safer our streets and emptier our prisons.

You may not be able to change the world, but you can change your little corner of it. A better compliment than "What an obedient child" is "What a responsible child you have raised."

BRINGING IT HOME

1. At what point does a child become accountable for specific behaviors?

2. When do behavioral monkeys jump from the child back to the parents?

3. How do you know when you have picked up too many monkeys?

4. What is the monkey-repellent phrase and what does it do?

5. In refusing to take back a specific monkey from a child, what does a parent empower the child to do?

MORAL MATURITY

Chapter Five

Moral Maturity— What Is It?

ne of the first challenges for parents is to discover what character traits they desire to see in their children. They also need to determine what traits they don't want to show up. This process is often facilitated by observation: We see attitudes we like and attitudes we don't like in children all around us.

Think about the teens you know. We have all met teens, preteens, and even younger children with whom we enjoy spending time. They are sociable, courteous, respectful, gracious, motivated, and genuine. They come from families where love between parent and child is evidenced by their mutual respect and by the absence of rebellious conflict.

How did these families get to the place of relational harmony? What is it about these kids that makes being with them enjoyable? What allows you to have fun with them (and them with you) without having to stoop to a buddy status? In our experience, there seems to be a common thread between them: These children possess moral maturity that makes being with them a pleasure.

When we say a child possesses moral maturity, this does not mean he or she is all-knowing and all-wise. Certainly that is not the case. This does mean, however, that the preteen has come to a place in which the values Mom and Dad have been communicating for so many years have at last been internalized.

It should begin to happen soon. Let's look at the steps you'll take in leading your middle-years child to moral maturity. To aid us in the process, we will take a story out of our earlier book, *On Becoming Childwise,* and expand on it here. The young lady in our story is now thirteen, wonderfully mature and delightful.

Elena's Story

On one occasion, Gary interviewed eight-year-old Elena, who was seeking entrance to a private school. To maximize educational excellence, the administrators of this school were as concerned about moral readiness as they were with academic preparation.

Gary posed a hypothetical moral question to Elena: "If you were sitting on a bus and all the seats were taken, and an older person came on the bus looking for a seat, what would you do?"

Elena put her head down for a moment, processed the question, and then offered this response. "It all depends," she said. "If there were a sign on the bus that required children to stay seated while the bus was in motion, then I would scoot over and ask the person to sit next to me. But if there were no sign, I would get up and let the person have my seat. Both ways, I would honor age."

Elena's answer is amazing on a number of levels. But what is perhaps most astounding is her introduction of a new element: a sign requiring that children remain seated while the bus is in motion. By adding this element, she created a condition in which two competing values of equal weight called for Elena's simultaneous attention: obedience to authority, represented by the sign, and respect for the elderly, derived from her parents' Judeo-Christian heritage. In the face of these seemingly conflicting values, her eight-year-old mind processed all the variables and came up with a way to satisfy both values without compromising either.

How is such moral insight gained? And what role do parents play in cultivating or delaying healthy moral attitudes? Here are four moral precepts to consider.

1. Moral training begins in parents' hearts.

Moral training begins with Mom and Dad. Effective parents know they cannot lead their child any further than they have gone themselves. If the prescription for moral living is not written on the parents' hearts, it will never be passed on to their children.

Bear in mind that a parent with advanced moral knowledge is not automatically a moral person. A moral lifestyle is not the automatic result of moral knowledge; it's a separate package entirely. Knowing right from wrong and doing the right thing are different things.

Personal integrity remains one of the great credibility builders of parenthood. Hypocrisy, on the other hand, destroys credibility every time. Parental hypocrisy occurs when Mom and Dad exempt themselves from values they require of their children. It's a breeding ground for contempt.

The moral rules we require our children to follow must also

apply to us. Keep that in mind. There can be no double standard in the upright home. A father cannot lecture on honesty and then when the phones rings say to his wife, "Tell them I'm not home." A mother mustn't require that her child respect authority, then go ballistic when a policeman pulls her over for driving too fast.

The truth is, our children will live at the same moral level we do, no matter what level we describe with our lips. As parents, we must continually be growing in our own moral sensitivity. Actively applying virtues and values in our own lives legitimizes the instruction we give our kids. This is especially important for readers of this book because in the middle years, your kids are watching every move you make. Slow down and take a moral inventory. Remember that old proverb, "When training children, more is caught than taught."

2. Know the why of moral training.

Many preadolescents know how to do all the right things in a variety of circumstances, but not as many know the why of their behavior. Knowing *how* to do right and *why* they should do it are two different things. The first represents an action; the second represents the principle behind the action.

Often children are taught what they should not do (e.g., do not steal) or should do (e.g., share your game with your sister). However, parents in our society consistently fail to teach the moral or practical *why* of behavior. This results in children who are outwardly moral, but not inwardly. They know how to respond in different circumstances because they have been trained, but they cannot adapt to unforeseen situations because they do not grasp the underlying moral principle.

Like Elena, Robby went through a moral readiness interview at the same private school. "Robby," Gary said, "imagine that you and your family are eating dinner at Mr. and Mrs. Brown's house. After dinner, Mrs. Brown brings out a beautiful cake and starts to pass out pieces to everyone, including herself. She then takes the cake and returns it to the kitchen. When would you start eating your piece of cake?"

"After Mrs. Brown sat down and started to eat her dessert." His answer speaks to the moral behavior insisted upon by his parents.

Next Gary asked a more specific question: "Robby, tell us why you would wait."

What would you expect his answer to be? Perhaps something along the lines of, "Because that's the way my parents taught me to do it." But Robby's parents had taught him the *why* of moral behavior. "My parents taught me to never be rude," he said. "It would be rude not to wait for the one who served us." Here is a child who is in the process of becoming morally mature.

It is not enough to teach your children how to act morally; they must learn how to think morally.

If a moral virtue is to take hold within a child, it must be placed there. Then the child must actually interact with the virtue. Little is accomplished by a one-way lecture about how a child should act.

Does this precept obligate you to provide a *why* explanation every time you correct your middle-years child? Of course not. Sometimes no just has to be no, even for a middle-years child. But, in order to reinforce the *why* behind the no, you should strive to tie your instructions to moral or practical reasons.

3. Provide the why of practical training.

Not every explanation offered by parents will be associated with moral training. Some explanations serve only a practical purpose. As a general rule, parents should offer a moral reason when a situation concerns people and a practical reason when a situation relates to things.

For example, Shayla's dad was killing weeds near the fruit tree. His busyness attracted her curiosity. Seeing his daughter draw near, he said, "Shayla, stay away from the tree, honey. I just sprayed poison around the trunk, and it's not safe."

In this situation, there was a practical reason (health and safety) why Shayla's behavior needed to be restrained, not a moral one. Since Shayla received practical information about what was going on at the tree, her curiosity was not further aroused. That information minimized the tension between Shayla's desire to obey and her natural curiosity.

4. Make moral judgments by examining context.

After morning service, some of the fourth-grade boys began to ride their bikes on the church patio where chuchgoers were milling about. When Ryan handed his Sunday school papers to his dad and headed toward his bike, his father stopped him and asked his intentions.

"I'm going to ride around the church with the guys," Ryan told him.

"Ryan," his dad said, "I'm going to ask you not to do that."

Then he did what is characteristic of responsible parenthood: He gave his son the moral reason why. Ryan's father looked into the context of the moment. Certainly there is nothing morally right or wrong about riding a bike. But there is something wrong about riding a bike on a crowded patio. One of the greatest skills to acquire in parenting is learning how to recognize and discern the moral significance of any situation.

Ryan's dad explained that riding on the church patio was not appropriate because of the presence of others. He was making Ryan aware of the world around him. He pointed out mothers with their babies, senior citizens coming and going (some with canes), folks in wheelchairs, and people who had hot coffee in their hands. He helped Ryan see the potential danger and explained why riding his bike in such circumstances was not being considerate of others.

This time, Dad governed Ryan's behavior. Next time, Ryan will be expected to do so on his own, because the principle has been placed in his heart.

To further illustrate the importance of giving your kids the moral reason behind your instructions and restrictions, let's extend this hypothetical situation a bit farther. Let's assume that Ryan's father denied him the opportunity to ride with his friends, but never gave the moral reason why. We have found that when no is given without explanation, kids view the rule as applying only for today. Next week, when Ryan's friends once again invite him to ride around the patio, Ryan will have no good reason *not* to ride, because no moral reason was placed in his heart. If there is no principle to stir the heart, it will not be stirred. That is when you end up with a robotic child who can go through all the right motions, but lack the type of morality that allows him to think and act on personal conviction. The absence of conviction only leaves children vulnerable to peer pressure.

SUMMARY

It is not enough to teach your children how to act morally; they must learn to think morally. Knowing the reason for virtuous conduct prevents robotic behavior. Children who do all the right things without knowing why are moral automatons. They often respond to situations and circumstances correctly, but not from any guiding principles of the heart.

In contrast, children who govern their behavior by moral principles are anything but robots. They are morally free, governing their behavior by intrinsic principle, not extrinsic circumstances. Getting the heart involved in life choices will be an invaluable asset in adolescence. It is a prerequisite to leading your middle-years child by your influence.

BRINGING IT HOME

1. When teaching moral principles, parents will often tell their children what is wrong and what not to do, but forget to talk about what is right and what they should do. What is wrong with this practice?

2. With whom does moral training begin. Why?

3. What is the difference between knowing *how* to do right and *why* it is right?

4. Based on the illustration of Ryan's riding his bike on the patio, explain what happens when parents fail to give a child the moral reason behind their instructions.

Chapter Six

Yes, They Still Need Correction

There's no doubt that young lives require training. That is the reason we discipline our children. They must learn to live safely, wisely, and in a manner respectful of those around them. Part of this guidance comes from encouraging right behavior, and part comes by correction. Correction means to bring back from error, or to realign an unacceptable deviation to the standard.

Certain fixed principles and practical truths guide the correction aspect of discipline. In this chapter we present some practical concepts that can help any parent bring correction to the life of a middle-years child. We'll start with the basics.

DISTINGUISH BETWEEN CHILDISHNESS AND DEFIANCE

You're standing there with your mouth wide open. The dollar toll begins to add up in your brain. Of course you warned him to be careful. But did you put enough steam in that warning to really count? At the age of nine, should he have known better? Perhaps, with all the cars parked in the field, this was neither the time nor the place for young Robby to be playing rock parachute. An egg-sized dent in your neighbor's new car makes you wish you had stopped this game long before now.

Where is the line between innocent play and malicious behavior? At what point does a misdemeanor become a felony? When do wrong actions become malicious disobedience?

If parenting were all about drawing lines, we would quickly run out of chalk. Fortunately, a thick black line has already been drawn for us in permanent ink. It marks the border between two totally separate realms of behavior. On one side is the land of childish mistakes; on the other is the land of defiant misdeeds. While the two realms have similar names, the difference between them is profound. The first speaks of non-rebellious acts; the second speaks of acts committed with malicious intent. Both require correction, but different kinds.

Let's look at the words *childishness* and *defiance*. We use the term *childishness* to refer to innocent immaturity. Childishness is when a child does something wrong, but wouldn't have if she'd been able to prevent it (accidents) or had known it was wrong. This includes those nonmalicious, nonrebellious, accidental mistakes our children make, such as spilling a glass of water, accidentally bumping another person, or picking fruit from a neighbor's tree. *Defiance,* on the other hand, implies bad motives. The child knew the act was wrong, but did it anyway.

Childishness is usually a head problem—a lack of knowledge. Defiance is usually a heart problem—the child does not want to do right.

Nine-year-old Nate sneaked into the house looking for a good hiding place. As he was going from room to room with childish glee, his foot caught a wire, and a porcelain lamp crashed to the floor. Promptly, all the children were gathered together and told that the inside of the house was off-limits for hide-and-seek. With nods of understanding, they all went back outside. Twenty minutes later, Nate's six-year-old sister, Nicole, came sneaking into the house looking for a place to hide.

Now, Nicole did exactly what her brother did, right? Nate had entered the house playing hide-and-seek, and so had she. But there's a huge difference. Nate did it in childish innocence; Nicole did it knowing full well it was wrong. She did it out of defiance.

Motives are the bridge from childishness to defiance. When parents have given instructions about something, and children have received them, there is little room for "innocent mistakes" regarding that behavior. If the child does the wrong thing intentionally, it's outright defiance, pure and simple.

Parents should correct both childishness and defiance. But the forms of correction differ. When assessing a behavior in need of correction, parents should ask themselves, *Was my child's action the result of an accident, a misunderstanding, or a lack of knowledge; or was it purposeful defiance with intent to cause harm?* How that question is answered will determine what happens next.

ALL CORRECTION MUST PROMOTE LEARNING

Correction requires explanation. Without the "why" of the wrong, there is no correction, just random redirection of behavior. The parent's job is to move the child from what he did this time to what he should do next time. Whatever the wrong, use it to impart knowledge. If you complete your talk and learning didn't take place, correction didn't happen. Consider the behavioral explanation you give today to be a deposit for tomorrow's behavior. Your goal is to transfer the impetus for right moral behavior from the external (you) to the internal (your child). That cannot happen without the "why" of behavior.

Having studied child-rearing patterns over the years, we have discovered that parents tend to spend more time and energy suppressing wayward behavior than elevating good behavior in their children. That is, when teaching life skills, parents will often tell their children what is wrong and what not to do instead of what is right and what they should be doing.

This kind of training seriously compromises learning in the future. Because so much emphasis is placed on which behaviors to avoid and too little on which ones to pursue, the path to virtuous deeds is not marked out for the child. If all you do is describe bad behavior, the only thing your child has a mental image of is bad behavior.

Twelve-year-old Sandy tormented her younger sister, Cheryl, in many ways. Sandy would tell her friends secrets, but she would publicly exclude Cheryl from these private talks. When the two girls rode bikes together, Sandy would cause Cheryl to fall off and get hurt. She would manipulate situations to gain an advantage over her sister, often at the expense of Cheryl's feelings. The girls' mother punished Sandy on each occurrence, but she could not understand why such exaggerated one-sided sibling conflict continued.

This mother failed to provide Sandy with a model of proper

behavior. Temporarily suppressing Sandy's waywardness by correcting her only perpetuated the problem. Mom focused so much on unkind behavior that she failed to teach the necessity of being kind. She did not provide Sandy with a picture of what kindness to her sister might look like.

Sandy needed clear suggestions and encouragement for demonstrating love for her sister. "Sandy, why don't you give your little sister a hug every morning?" "Sandy, maybe you could take some time to teach Cheryl a new skill." "Sandy, next time why not play the game Cheryl suggests?"

Restraining morally wrong behavior and encouraging morally right behavior are two sides of the same coin. Parents must teach both if learning is to take place in their children.

CORRECT PERSONAL ATTITUDES THROUGH SUBSTITUTION

Not long ago a young father said to Gary, "My son has a problem with jealousy. How do I punish him?" This question leads to a broader one. How do you correct any hurtful attitude of the heart?

Because of their age, middle-years children are better served by substitution than suppression. The father mentioned above was frustrated by his failed efforts to suppress his son's jealousy. No matter how hard Dad tried to keep the lid on it, jealousy continued to leak out. Instead of attempting to suppress the moral shortcoming, he needed to enhance the opposite virtue.

If you have a child struggling with selfishness, teach generosity; with anger, teach self-control; with revenge, teach forgiveness. The young father finally did that, and his son's jealousy gave way to a sense of contentment.

TEACH TOMORROW'S CONSEQUENCES TODAY

Teach your children concretely by showing them tomorrow's consequences for today's decisions. The operative word is *concretely*. There are some lessons that our children must absorb through their senses or experience if they are to learn them.

Katie and Matt, although fun to play with, had not been trained to be responsible children. The Ezzo kids knew that from previous experience. One Saturday afternoon while Katie and Matt were visiting Amy and Jenny, the four decided to play house. But instead of playing upstairs in the girls' rooms, Katie and Matt convinced Amy and Jenny to set up house outside in the woods.

The Ezzos gave their children one warning: "Girls, everything you take out must be returned."

"Okay, Mom and Dad."

The parents knew how this was going to turn out. Their girls should have known, too.

Amy, Jenny, Katie, and Matt began hauling small tables and chairs, play stoves, and play sinks to the woods alongside the house. Before long, an Alice in Wonderland tea party had begun under a natural canopy of oak and maple trees. The kids had neatly placed little plates, knives, forks, and napkins on the table. The "kitchen" had pans on the make-believe stove, dishes beside the pretend sink, and rocking chairs filled with stuffed animals.

They had been playing for about ten minutes when Matt and Katie's mom called them home. Amy and Jenny asked Katie and Matt to help them return everything to the house. Matt and Katie greeted their request with an uncharacteristic desire to obey their mother immediately. "We gotta go. Our mother is calling." In that moment, the girls realized their mistake. Their guests left and they had to put every item away by themselves.

The girls' parents could have helped. They could have come alongside the girls, picked up some of their toys, and tried to use the moment to teach. But they purposely chose not to. They wanted this lesson to sink in.

They directed the girls to return everything to their rooms and put their playthings back where they belonged. When they were done, the Ezzos sat and talked about unreliable friends. The girls had already discerned that Katie and Matt were unreliable, yet they had not acted on what they knew. Every trip back to their rooms helped reinforce a lesson that would serve them for life.

Teach your middle-years children by showing them concretely tomorrow's consequences for today's decisions.

UNDERSTAND HOW BOYS AND GIRLS COMMUNICATE DIFFERENTLY

There are many influences on successful communication with children. Age, personality, temperaments, and even birth order of both parent and child help shape the construction of thought and understanding. Gender is yet another factor, especially with children ages nine and above. Age nine seems to be the biological signpost announcing the onset of gender differences. These differences affect both communication and understanding—especially when we are trying to make a point with our children.

For example, preadolescent boys tend to feel more comfortable with *indirect* conversation when receiving corrections, while preadolescent girls tend to feel more comfortable with *direct* discussion.

Consider boys of this age. If a father confronts his son face-to-face, the natural response will be defensiveness.

"Son, Mom has informed me that your attitude toward your sister is troubling to everyone in the family. We need to deal with this problem."

That type of direct approach often produces a self-protective response. "Dad, that's not true. I didn't do it."

The in-your-face approach to problem solving often leads to greater problems such as denial, or weak masculinity. Boys simply do not do well with unannounced direct confrontation.

So try the indirect approach. Instead of sitting down face-to-face with your son, let him know that the two of you are going to be working on the car engine. While you're changing the plugs or replacing belts, bring up the problem of his attitude. You'll be amazed at how easy it is to talk about something touchy when you are both working on a neutral project. This is the indirect method.

Parents who practice this report amazing success. They find that not only do their sons tend to listen in a nondefensive posture, but that they also tend to act on the correction much more readily than if the parents had gone at the problem head-on.

Preadolescent girls are just the opposite. They do not do well when other activities are taking place at the moment of conversation. For example, if a mother and daughter are washing dishes together and something important comes up, the dishes will sit there unwashed. If they're going to talk, they'll talk.

Girls tend to feel more comfortable with direct conversation. They will tend to receive correction better if the two take cups of hot chocolate, sit together on the couch, and talk face-to-face and heart-to-heart.

UNDERSTAND MICRO- AND MACROREBELLION

Rebellion can be defined as willful defiance. This includes disobedience, back talk, refusal to accept correction, and rejection of rightful authority.

Most kids demonstrate open rebellion. When they cross the line, they cross it all the way. We call this *macrorebellion*. For example, you tell your son to put the ball down gently, but instead he throws it at his sister. Or you call your child to come to you, and he runs off in the opposite direction.

There are a number of children who rebel in more subtle ways, content to put just one toe over the line. The action of these children fall into the microrebellion category. That is, their defiance is not as openly challenging as that of the macrorebel. The microrebel is one who, instead of running away when called, will come halfway to you. This is the child who, when asked to put the ball down, will put it in his or her pocket. When asked to stay out of the kitchen, a microrebel will place both heels on the carpet and ten toes just across the floor tiles.

One distinguishing characteristic of this child is that he or she rarely rebels on a large scale. And that becomes part of the problem. The wrong of the microrebel just doesn't look as bad when compared to that of openly rebellious siblings. Thus, parents tend to underestimate the seriousness of the offense, dismissing it as just another minor infraction. However, it is not a minor infraction to the child. For the microrebel, the toe over the line is one hundred percent rebellion. The toe may be only partly over the line, but your child's heart is completely over it.

Rebellion, uncorrected, leads to contempt for authority. If you have a microrebellious child who is still in the middle years, work diligently to correct his defiance. If you don't, the consequences will show up during the teen years.

DO NOT PARENT TO THE LOWEST COMMON DENOMINATOR

"I'm afraid if I ease the restrictions on my oldest child," one mother said, "the younger children will not understand why they don't have the same privileges."

This attitude is all too common. Instead, Mom needs to tell the younger children that when they become as responsible as their older brother or sister, they too will have those special privileges.

It is necessary to grant freedoms to your child as he or she attains the age-appropriate level of self-control. Granting freedoms to a child that are greater or lesser than the child's capacity for self-control creates a state of developmental imbalance. If you withhold a freedom from a child who is developmentally and morally ready for it, you cause frustration, just as you do if you give freedoms to a child who is not ready for them.

> freedoms granted that are greater or lesser than a child's level of
> self-control = developmental frustration

Withholding freedom from a child who possesses age-appropriate self-control will eventually foster frustration. The child has the knowledge and ability to be responsible, but his parents have not given him the freedom to apply these attributes. This situation indicates that Mom and Dad are being over-controlling.

We understand why parents are tempted to respond in this way. It is easy to lead by control, particularly if you have younger children in your home. If all of your kids are in the teen years, or all are in the middle years, there is not quite as much tension. But if you still have toddlers or children around five or six, you still need to use parental authority with them.

If this is the case in your home, it is tempting to treat your older ones the same way as you do the younger ones. This is parenting to the lowest common denominator, and it is not in the best interests of your middle-years child.

When you are working with children at differing age levels, you are constantly changing hats. Parenting to the proper age level is not easy, but it is vital to your children's growth. Many parents frustrate their middle-years children by shackling them with the restraints they place on the younger siblings.

In one of the Ezzos' recent parenting conferences, this subject came up when a mother said that she makes her nine-year-old go to bed when she tucks in her five-year-old.

"Why?" the Ezzos asked.

The mother was very candid. "Because if I didn't, I would have a bedtime battle on my hands with the little one. And I don't want that."

Please, Mom and Dad, don't do this to your middle-years child. Deal with the little brother; don't penalize the older child by withholding freedoms. Remember, you're transitioning away from authority-based parenting for your middle-years child. Younger children may wish for that transition, too, but for them it's not time yet.

SUMMARY

Many parents consider discipline a means of controlling a child's actions for the moment. That is only partially true. Actions taken for expediency now must be in harmony with the long-term objective: training up a young person who can survive (and thrive) independently in the teen years.

Are you starting to see some of this fruit in your middle-years child? Our earnest desire is that you will—soon.

BRINGING IT HOME

1. In your own words, distinguish between childishness and defiance.

2. In our story about Sandy, what mistakes did her mother make as she tried to suppress Sandy's cruelty to her younger sister?

3. Are you dealing with a recurring moral issue with your child now? What would be the virtue you could promote instead of simply clamping down on the problem?

4. How could you concretely teach your child a lasting lesson about the consequences of decisions?

5. Do you have a middle-years child who is a micro- or macrorebel? How is the rebellion demonstrated in his or her life?

6. Explain the following statement: Freedoms granted that are greater than or less than a child's level of self-control equals developmental frustration.

Chapter Seven

Moral Processing I:
The Spirit of the Law

O n the soccer field, ten-year-old Johnny's father accepts only the best. "Score it, Johnny!" Dad shouts from the sidelines. "Take it to the net, son. Go, John! Go!"

Many parents today want nothing but the best from their children for the life of a game, yet are all too willing to accept something less for them in the game of life. Johnny needs only smile when Uncle Joe shows up to watch his game. *Hey, the kid smiled,* thinks Dad. *Not bad; it's better than a belch.* Mediocrity as the standard for moral behavior has become the American way.

Here is a different Johnny. "Hi, Uncle Joe. I'm really glad you came to my game. That was really nice of you to drive over here to watch me." Ten-year-old Johnny not only extends a formal welcome, but demonstrates heartfelt appreciation for the sacrifice made on his behalf.

Not too many years ago, the Ezzos went to visit some associates in Tucson, Arizona. When they got out of the car, they noticed eight-year-old Timarie standing on the sidewalk, waiting for their arrival. They made eye contact with her and said, "Hello. Are you one of the Lambrose children?"

"Yes," she responded. Then she walked toward the Ezzos with adultlike confidence and put out her hand to shake theirs. As she graciously looked up into their eyes, she said with all sincerity, "Hello, Mr. and Mrs. Ezzo. It is very nice to meet you. Did you have a nice trip over to Tucson?"

Were they impressed? Yes, very much so. Timarie's interest in them was clearly genuine. It was not the result of a dress rehearsal a few minutes prior to their arrival. A few minutes later, the Ezzos met Timarie's siblings who, in their own way, demonstrated the same moral sensitivity. Later in the visit, they asked the parents what they had done to bring their children to this level of moral sincerity. They said they had taught their children three levels of moral responses: *good, better,* and *best.*

Good, better, best; never let it rest. Even the worst parent works to evoke *good* moral responses from a child, especially in the presence of strangers. Anything less is humiliating. In today's world, eliciting not just good, but *better* behavior from your child wins you praises. So it's all too easy to stop there. Yet *better* simply is not the best parents can expect from their children. With a slight increase in invested time and effort, you can give your children a moral legacy that spills over into all of society.

Teach your child the three levels of moral responses. Begin by explaining that behaving at the *good* level represents the minimum courtesy required in a moral situation. If someone says, "Hello," the least your child should do is acknowledge the greeter by saying

"Hello" in return. If the person extends a compliment, such as, "Your new haircut looks sharp," the minimum courtesy is to say, "Thank you."

Behaving in this way—at the level of *good*—represents the child himself. Explain that doing *better* represents your family. It speaks of who you are and what you stand for as a household.

Better takes us beyond the minimum to the next step: extending a courtesy. For example, encourage your children to reach out and shake hands with any adult to whom they are introduced. Stress the importance of looking a person in the eye while shaking hands. Also, you may want to teach your child that if he is sitting when a visitor walks into the room, he should stand and acknowledge the new-comer's presence. This demonstrates both kindness and respect.

Finally, doing what is *best* represents something much larger than just the family. It is a response based on a brotherly love that flows into all the world. Rather than simply saying "Hi" when someone extends a hand, the child initiates kindness. Not only would Johnny say "Hello" and walk toward Uncle Joe with his hand extended, but he would also initiate conversation. "I know you gave up your golf game to come watch me," he might say. "Will you get to play later?" Those few words go a long way. *Good* is acceptable; *better* is preferable; but *best*—seeking to meet the highest standard of moral response—is the most desirable.

An ancient proverb says that "even a child is known by his deeds, whether what he does is pure and right." A child's moral disposition will show itself. Just as the new bud leads to a blossom and the blossom leads to fruit, what is in your child's heart will some day blossom.

How can you move your son or daughter beyond an external compliance to the letter of the law to the pursuit of ethical excellence? Moral disposition shows itself through right principles that parents place in a child's heart. It is now time to take your middle-years child to the next level of moral sensitivity. Go beyond *good* and *better*. Encourage your preadolescent to strive for *best*—the excellencies found in a heart filled with brotherly love.

SELF-GENERATED INITIATIVE

Barb and Phil's five children, ranging in age from seven to fourteen, were all-around great kids. Each demonstrated kindness, great table manners, and self-control. Each responded politely when spoken to and was courteous to strangers. Yet Mom and Dad had an uneasy sense of a gap in their children's characters. There was something missing in their moral profiles that their parents could not identify.

In school, Barb and Phil's children would never knowingly drop a piece of paper on the floor and walk away from it. And if a teacher asked them to pick up a piece of paper lying on the floor, they would happily do so. But if the teacher did not instruct them to pick up the piece of paper, they would not have done it on their own. All five kids lacked *self-generated initiative*.

Self-generated initiative is the highest and most desirable level of moral motivation. At this level, a child responds to needs without prompting or instruction. This was what was missing in the children's moral profiles.

Most encouraging, however, was how quickly the problem was fixed. Barb and Phil realized they needed to teach their kids about self-generated initiative, through both conversation and action. All around the house they posted three-by-five cards on which these words were written: *Don't wait to be asked to do good before doing good.* In less than two weeks that slogan had paid big dividends. Self-generated initiative had become a part of their children's character.

THE SPIRIT OF THE LAW

During the middle years, children are able to understand so much more of how things work in this world. Their intellectual abilities are developing quickly and they are as teachable as they will ever be.

This is your opportunity to change how you parent your preadolescent. No longer do you just say no; now you begin to teach the principle behind the no. What a wonderful development! Now you instill in your child the reason for the no so that when a similar situation arises, she's got the principle in her moral repertoire, ready to be applied. This is what parenting in these years is all about. When the teen years come, everything that can be pre-loaded in your child had better already be there.

Falling out of Bed

When Jerry's dad said, "Stay in bed, son, and leave the light off," he was expecting total compliance. But when Jerry's little brother fell out of bed in the middle of the night, Jerry got up and turned on a light in order to help him. Wasn't he acting in open defiance of his father's wishes?

Definitely not. Jerry understood his father's instructions. He understood the context and the purpose for which they were given.

He knew it was not his father's intent for him to stay in bed under any circumstances.

Jerry could have obeyed the letter of the law and stayed in bed. But to have done so would have compromised the greater need of the moment—comforting his younger brother and helping him back into bed. Not only would the greater good have been compromised, but his failure to provide comfort to a frightened sibling would have created a greater wrong. Given these options, he chose to respond according to the principle behind the instruction.

Jerry was able to regulate his behavior because he was trained to the principle, not the letter of the law. More than that, he possessed a healthy degree of self-generated initiative. He did not wait until he heard from the other room, "Jerry, help your brother." Rather, he acted on his moral knowledge and did what he knew was right.

Your middle-years child, too, must step beyond external obedience. To help your child achieve this level of sensitivity, you must move him or her:

- from outward compliance to the letter of the law;
- to inward understanding of the principle behind the law;
- to a place where he can automatically apply the principle to other situations.

AS EASY AS...CAKE

Dave and Kim were looking forward to a visit from their old friends, Larry and Sue. Kim had baked Larry's favorite cake for that night's dessert. After she applied the special maple frosting,

Kim placed the cake on the kitchen table. She turned to ten-year-old Nate, who was sitting at the counter working on a puzzle, and said, "Now, Nate, don't take a swipe of frosting with your finger. In fact, I don't want you to touch the cake at all. It's a surprise dessert for Mr. Miller. I'm going next door, but I'll be back in half an hour."

Kim left the kitchen, and Nate continued working his puzzle. A few minutes later he noticed that the angle of the sunlight was changing. Hot rays began to stream in through the window and fall on the cake. He soon realized that if the cake wasn't moved, the frosting would melt and the dessert would be ruined.

Nate was confronted with a moral decision. The letter of the law said, "Don't touch the cake at all." But the intent of the law had also been made known: "It's a surprise dessert for Mr. Miller." The intent was communicated as part of the instructions, and that is what Nate finally acted on.

He respected his mother's order, but he also considered what she really meant by it. She didn't mean that he could touch it under no circumstances, only that he was not to eat any of it. She wanted the cake to remain intact because it was a gift for the Millers. Understanding the principle behind the law gave Nate the freedom to do what was right without fear. In order to protect his mother's feelings and wishes, he got up and moved the cake out of the sun's rays.

He could have done nothing and still have met the letter of the law. But like Jerry in our previous illustration, he did what was *best,* or morally superior.

SUMMARY

Imagine that your ten-year-old is supervising younger siblings and their school friends while you hold a brief community meeting in your home. He's doing well, keeping the younger ones involved in an informal soccer game. Then Jill and her parents arrive. Your son notices Jill watching silently from the sidelines because she is wearing a white dress and shiny black shoes.

What does he do? What should he do?

One thing he might do, if he were learning how to be morally mature, would be to do something that would allow Jill to participate in the group, such as suggesting an activity in which everyone could take part. This type of responsible action first requires a moral knowledge of what is right and then the conviction to act on that knowledge.

Your middle-years child should be in the process of acquiring a set of personal values to which she adheres with increasing frequency. She should understand what is good, better, and best—and she should be striving to act in accordance with the best whenever possible. She should be able to take the intent of your instructions and apply them to situations as they arise.

If these things are taking place, you will have an extraordinarily wonderful relationship when your son or daughter reaches the teen years because you and your child will have the same set of values. While conflicting values war against intimate healthy relationships, but common values will bind your family together like nothing else can.

BRINGING IT HOME

1. Explain the three moral responses of *good*, *better*, and *best*.

2. What is self-generated moral initiative?

3. The next time you give your child an instruction, listen to what you say. Do you explain the principle behind your instructions?

4. Test your teaching and your child's learning by giving a hypothetical situation and asking him how you might want him to respond.

Chapter Eight

Moral Processing II:
The Appeals Process

Standing at the top of the basement stairs, Steve calls down to his son, "Hey, Harrison, tomorrow we're going to hit the slopes early, so come on up and get ready for bed."

What is Harrison to do? He has every intergalactic space creature he owns scattered on the floor and a dozen Jedi knights prepared to rush three newly erected space stations. Dad's instructions couldn't have come at a worse time. Abandoning this fantastic battle scenario would invite an invasion from younger siblings bent on destroying his tiny model universe. To obey or not to obey, that is the question. He's on the horns of a dilemma.

Your middle-years child is developing the ability to think logically. Parents usually discover this when their child points up a logical contradiction they have made. (The unsettling thing about it is that the child is often right!) Though you might not believe it at the time, this development really is a good thing. It goes hand in hand with his newfound ability to understand the reasons behind your instructions. Now your child knows that it is sometimes right to disobey what Mom and Dad have said in order to obey what they meant.

You, Mom or Dad, have to understand that sometimes you can give an instruction to your child that puts him in a corner because of circumstances of which you are unaware. You need to be willing to listen to reasonable objections.

TEACHING THE APPEALS PROCESS

Neither extreme of parenting—overauthoritarian or overindulgent—has any use for an appeals process. As far as the overauthoritarian parent is concerned, he's always right—even when he's wrong. The child cannot be allowed to challenge the parent's absolute authority, for fear that it would lead to anarchy and rebellion. The overindulgent parent, on the other hand, always gives in to the child anyway, so who needs an appeals process? That parent might actually want the right of appeal—for himself!

For those between these extremes, an appeals process can help bring your authority into focus. To appeal to authority is to acknowledge another's rule in our lives. To be in a position of leadership and to hear an appeal is to accept human imperfection.

Remember, none of us is a perfect parent. We all make errors in judgment. Yes, we desire that our children submit to our leadership without grumbling, murmuring, or disputing. But submission is a difficult task for all of us. In parenting, we must be especially sensitive to this fact throughout the training process or we risk exasperating our children.

A parent who asks a preteen to turn off the movie five minutes before its conclusion or to put away a game when it is nearly over exasperates his child, and frustrates him unnecessarily.

Unnecessarily is the operative word. Parenting, by definition, frustrates children. What are parents but those who, among their many activities, tell the child what he cannot do? They restrict the free expression of the child's nature. But there is a difference between the right and wrong expression of authority. It is right for police to patrol the streets; police brutality or harassment is wrong. Correction is necessary; exasperation is not.

Just because your child gets frustrated when you call him inside, insist that he take off his muddy shoes, or request that he be kind to his sister doesn't mean you should stop giving him instructions. What parents must guard against is the unnecessary frustrations they can create by delivering instructions inappropriately. Unfortunately, at times all of us are insensitive or don't know the whole situation.

So how can parents maintain order in the home without exasperating their children? The answer is found in the appeals process—giving a child who has received an instruction the chance to provide *new information* that will cause a parent to rethink the instruction.

In the appeals process, the preteen proactively provides new information that will help the parent reconsider previous instruction. Saying, "Mom, I don't want to" is not giving new information. It is stating a preference. The appeals process is designed to alert a parent to a different reference point—that of the child.

Caleb was watching an auto racing video that had five minutes left to run. His mom didn't realize how close it was to the end and told her son to turn off the television and wash up for dinner. In this case, her frame of reference was dinner, which she was about to put on the table. Caleb's frame of reference was the video, which was near completion.

Should Caleb comply by leaving the program, but be frustrated? Or should he ignore his mother in order to satisfy his desire to watch the conclusion of the race? Either way, Caleb would be exasperated. He doesn't want to miss the end of the movie, but he doesn't want to do battle with his mother's authority either.

The appeals process bridges the two extremes, preventing both disobedience and exasperation.

WHEN AND HOW?

To activate an appeal, the preadolescent, not the parent, must initiate the process by providing new information. The parent's part is to hear the new information and, if appropriate, reconsider her instructions. An appeal is not always granted. There may be new information, but it may not be relevant. Yes, no, and maybe are all possible responses to an appeal. But the child's perspective will have been considered, and that's usually all he wants.

In Caleb's case, he could appeal his mom's instruction by saying, "Mom, may I give you new information? There are only five minutes left on the video. May I finish it first?" With this information, his mom may reconsider the request without compromising her leadership or what is best for the whole family.

There is a legitimacy to his appeal and probably no reason why she would not change and say, "Yes, that's fine. When it is done, please wash up for dinner." There is no exasperation, no conflict, and no power struggle. Now everyone wins.

Conflict in the Bleachers

Bob and his family found seats together at a ball game, but Christopher, age twelve, sat several seats away. Bob instructed him to move closer and heard, "No, Dad, I want to sit here!" Christopher's answer challenged his parents' authority and thereby created conflict. If Bob repeated himself, he would reinforce Christopher's noncompliance. If he gave in, he would be compromising his authority and parental integrity. Christopher's unqualified refusal forced Bob to take corrective measures.

After receiving a verbal admonishment, Christopher explained his frame of reference. "Dad, I sat over there because I couldn't see all the players with that banner hanging so low." Was that a legitimate reason to sit away from the family? Yes. Was it handled the best way? No. If Christopher's parents had taught him how to appeal properly, the entire negative scene would have been avoided.

The appeal process would have brought peace to the situation without compromise or frustration. Upon receiving instructions, Christopher would have moved near to his dad and asked, "May I appeal?" That simple question would have set the proper course of events in motion. Having received new information about the low, hanging banner, Bob could have reconsidered his son's legitimate request.

During this paricular crisis, the father realized the power of the appeal process. By using it, parents can elminate many unnecessary conflicts without compromising their authority or violating their relationship with their children.

were two baskets of clean clothes in the base-
he children home from school, Jan said, "As
soon as you kids change your clothes, I want you to go down to the
basement and fold and put away your laundry." Both children did
exactly as Mom instructed. Meanwhile, their dad came home and
asked, "Why are those trash barrels still on the street? I told the kids
to put them in the garage as soon as they got home."

When two authorities give instructions that require simultaneous responses, a problem naturally arises. The child cannot win: To
obey one parent means disobeying the other. How could this have
been handled better? Had appeals process training taken place, the
children would have felt free to say, "Mom, may we give you new
information? Dad told us to bring the barrels in from the street as
soon as we came home. Which task do you want us to do first?"
Jan, having received the new information, would have been free to
reexamine her instructions without compromising her authority or
her husband's instructions.

If she had instructed her children to do the laundry first, then
she would have been responsible for explaining the situation to
Dad when he came home. Without the opportunity to appeal, obedience can become anxious and confusing and sometimes lead to
unfair punishment.

GUIDELINES FOR MAKING AN APPEAL

The appeals process is often misused. To prevent that, consider
these seven basic guidelines.

Guideline One

The appeals process is for children who are old enough to understand its purpose. This is a tool for your two- or three-year-old. Children five years old and older can quickly grasp the concept.

Guideline Two

The appeal must only be made to the parent currently giving the instructions. That is, if Dad is instructing, the child is not to appeal to Mom. That would only undermine the authority of both parents. To demonstrate parental unity, neither parent should receive an appeal from a child who has not first gone to the initiating parent.

Guideline Three

Parents should entertain an appeal only when the child comes in humility. A gentle spirit communicates the child's recognition of his parents' right to rule and overrule. "Why can't I?" "Do I have to?" and, "But Mom!" are not appeals, but challenges to authority. No humility, no appeal. The appeal must also be made face-to-face, not shouted from one room to another.

Guideline Four

Appeals can only be made once. In other words, a child cannot repeatedly plead his case. "But Dad, but Dad, but Dad!" and "Please may I, please may I, please may I?" are not permissible. The child must learn to accept no gracefully and to do as told. That will happen when the child learns that his parents are trustworthy and that they will listen to legitimate appeals.

Guideline Five

Start by teaching your children to use an exact phrase, whatever that phrase might be for your family. "May I appeal?" or "May I give you some new information?" or "May I ask you to reconsider?" are all workable requests. Whichever one you use, stay with it. Its uniqueness draws attention to its purpose.

Guideline Six

The appeals process is a privilege, not a way to avoid objectionable tasks or personal responsibility. Do not ruin a good thing by letting your child appeal every decision you make. It is not to be used as a forum to state likes and dislikes.

Guideline Seven

If the appeals process is to work effectively, parents must be fair and flexible. Think about why you say no. Is there a good reason it cannot be yes?

HOW TO TEACH THE APPEALS PROCESS

Introduce the appeals process using the following three steps.

1. Sit down with your children and work through the principles, examples, and guidelines of this chapter.

2. Set up a few scenarios that might fit your family situation. In each one include an example of a correct and an incorrect way to make an appeal.

3. Once your children have mastered the concepts, test them. Allow the natural consequences of wrong choices to reinforce your training. If they come to you with a wrong attitude or if they fail to

bring new information, deny their appeal. If they start to appeal everything, take the privilege away for a while.

The appeals process is a matter of trust. The child trusts the parent to be fair and flexible, and the parent trusts the child to bring new information that legitimizes the appeal.

SUMMARY

So what ever happen to Harrison? In real life, nine-year-old Harrison came to the top of the stairs and asked his dad if he could make an appeal.

"Dad, I have all my space toys scattered all over the floor. That's the room the little kids are going to sleep in. May I have five more minutes to put everything away before the kids go to bed?"

With that new information, Harrison's dad granted his son's request. No frustration, tension, or shouting. Everyone won, without compromising Dad's leadership or sending Harrison off to bed frustrated.

In general, life is not fair. Children are not the parents; they don't get to make the rules. Nor do you as parents control all the events of your own lives. That's the way the world is. But you can alleviate some of the tension in your corner of it by using the appeals process.

We are all willing to submit to authority to the degree that the authority is trustworthy and, as far as possible, fair. Being willing to listen to your middle-years child's legitimate appeals shows you are an authority figure worthy of trust and obedience. That's one more tie binding your family together as your child approaches the teen years.

BRINGING IT HOME

1. List advantages of the appeals process for your family.

2. Think about the last month and write down an incident in which the appeals process would have benefited the situation.

3. Do the steps listed in "How to Teach the Appeals Process."

SECTION THREE

FAMILY IDENTITY

Chapter Nine

Building Family Identity

*I*magine yourself on a boat for a week drifting ever so calmly with—yikes!—your own mom and dad. Joining you are your grown siblings and—gulp—their spouses and kids.

You're probably imagining a comedy or a horror flick. Yet not long ago, the senior Ezzos were the grandparents in that exact scenario. For a week Gary and Anne Marie, their two married daughters, and their families enjoyed Lake Meade on a rented houseboat. They swam, fished, read, relaxed, and in general had an incredibly good time. So good, in fact, that on the journey home the girls were already planning for the next time.

Friendship with your adult children is a parenting dividend you don't give much thought to when you are changing diapers, giving baths, or reading bedtime stories. But as your children grow, it's important to ask: "When my children become old enough to select their own friends, will they have any reason to choose us or their sisters and brothers? Do my children consider members of their family part of their inner circle of most loyal friends?"

If you have a strong family identity, the answers to these questions can be yes.

Family identity is critically important as a child begins to enter the teen years. Children who receive comfort and approval from a close-knit family tend to look to those same or similar relationships as they move through adolescence. Within the comfortable confines of such a family, it is parents, not peers, who usually have the greater influence.

The nature of progressive development reveals that children (especially teens) choose their peer friends only after they either accept or reject their family identity. If they accept the family as the primary source of values and comfort, then teens will make friends from among peers who possess similar values. This creates positive peer pressure. When there is harmony between the core beliefs of parents and children, children gravitate to families and friends with similar values.

On the other hand, a child who depends on outside influences for the satisfaction of basic social needs is more likely to grow up being sensitive to group pressures and disapproval. The tendency for these children is to move in the direction of peers and to become indifferent toward nonpeer influences, such as parents.

Peer pressure on a child is only as strong as family identity is weak. We'll discuss peer pressure in detail in the next chapter, but for now know that building a strong family identity will reduce negative peer pressure on your child. *You* want to be the source of your child's acceptance, affection, and values. Now, how do you become that?

Even in the closest of human relationships, such as that of a parent and child, there is no guarantee of future rapport. Though both parties contribute to the outcomes in the relationship, for the most part, parents remain in the driver's seat. They greatly influence the outcome by the choices they make.

One such choice deals with family structure. Are you an interdependent or an independent family? The first is extremely desirable, even necessary. The second is dangerous. Let's look closely at each.

INTERDEPENDENT VS. INDEPENDENT FAMILY STRUCTURE

Please take note of the prefix *inter* in the word *interdependent*. Like two-by-fours in the frame of a house, each individual part supports the others in order to create a whole. The relationship of each board to the others is mutual. In the same way, each member of the interdependent family is dependent upon the others.

A group of people holding hands in a circle and facing inward is a symbolic illustration of the best possible way to send and receive family values. These values are communicated and demonstrated by Mom and Dad. They're sent to the children, shared with each other, and sent back again to Mom and Dad. In an interdependent family, the standards of moral conduct for each family member are established primarily within the home.*

An interdependent family provides satisfaction, protection, and security in a child's early years. It also serves as a barrier against

---

*Interdependency should not be confused with the popular counseling term *codependency*. When problems arise in interdependent relationships, the issue is confronted right away, and each individual seeks to restore the whole. When problems arise in codependent relationships, fear and insecurity produce behavior that covers up the issue and functions around it.

intrusive values, especially during a child's teen years. The inter-dependent family cultivates a sense of belonging that leads to allegiance to one another and to the core values of the family. Children grow with an attitude of "we-ism" regarding their family.

In contrast, an *independent* family structure leads to "me-ism." Each member of such a family is free from the influence, guidance, or control of another. That sounds attractive to our American sensibilities—the land of the free and all. But what it means in a family is that individual family members are unaffiliated, alienated, or not committed to one another. In short, they stand alone.

The independent family holds hands and stands in a circle. But instead of all members looking in toward one another, each member looks out, away from the center. They look unified from a distance, but it is far from being what it should be. Everyone is caught up in his own little world, doing his own independent thing. As a result, more by default than by choice, children turn to their peers for support, love, and values.

In theory most people would choose the interdependent family structure. Everyone wants to belong, to be supportive, and to be supported. But for the structure to work in real life, it means sacrifice. It means being there for one another.

The process begins with parents. We must be there for our family. There will always be better jobs, higher positions, and greater opportunities for enrichment. These are all good, and it is hard to say no to them. But when parents no longer make time to fulfill their role as the primary moral influence on their children, the resulting vacuum will be filled by other influences: media, public institutions, and peers.

The result can be nothing but increased alienation, indifference, and independence on the part of the children. You can't expect family harmony when other voices are instilling their values in your kids—values very often incompatible with yours.

Who is really raising your child? Here is a little test to help you determine which type of family you are and who has the greatest influence on your child.

- Excluding yourself and your spouse, what people spend at least one hour with your child during the course of a week?
- How many hours does each of those people spend with your child?
- How many hours per week does your child spend taking in the media (TV, movies, magazines, Internet, etc.)?
- How many of the people and media sources you have listed have standards and values that differ from your own?
- What is the total number of hours your child is exposed to these negative influences every week?

In relation to your child and his influences, what type of family are you? If this test reveals something you don't like, don't despair. Just consider how you might take steps in the right direction. The weaker the outside influences in the early and middle years, the less potential there is for division in the teen years.

BUILDING FAMILY IDENTITY TAKES TIME

Today, life seems to be speeding by faster than ever before. The pace of everything has seemingly accelerated, including the rate at which row. Within a few years, your middle-years child will ~~uoiescence, and your preadolescent will be on the brink of adulthood. When that happens, time will not be on your side. When your child is ready to leave the nest, will she have fond memories of the family interactions that anchor her to you?

Here are some practical suggestions to help you generate a healthy family identity.

Cultivate it.

If you want to build a trusting relationship with your children, start by cultivating attitudes that lead to a strong sense of family identity. Family identity is the mutual acceptance of who you are as a family. It is based on trust, acceptance, and a growing loyalty between members. It is a significant factor in the life of every child. It is the best defense against negative peer pressure.

In the Ezzo and Bucknam households, family ties were never optional. Each person knew the team was counting on every family member to stay committed to the code of ethics that represented the family. Consistent loyalty to our family values sealed our identity as a unit. Even today, whether together or apart, both families are committed to those mutual standards.

Verbalize your commitment to the family whenever appropriate. This is especially critical for fathers. Dad cannot be a mere spectator, observing Mom's efforts to hold the family together. Dad must be an active leader and participant in the process. We urge dads to verbalize their pleasure and excitement with their family. While driving in the car or sitting around the dinner table, encourage your family by making statements such as, "This is really a terrific family. I am so thankful we're together" or "You kids have the best mom in the world."

Why is such verbalization important? When Dad is excited and encouraged about the family, children feel the same way. It's an amazing phenomenon. But when Dad is silent about the family, the question lingers in their minds—"Does he really care about us?" You may think that by not talking, you are not communicating anything to your kids. Not so. With your silence you communicate disinterest, or worse, fatherly disapproval or rejection. Your child's confidence in you grows as he or she sees and hears that Dad is on board with the family.

Read after dinner.

Have your ever read the true-life adventures of Dr. Walter Reed and how he discovered how yellow fever was transmitted? Or about Booker T. Washington, the boy who had no last name until he gave himself one? Then there's Albert Schweitzer and his great work in Africa, Florence Nightingale, Clara Barton, Louis Pasteur, and George Washington Carver. These are more than legends from our past. These are great men and women of history whose life stories are packed with examples of courage, perseverance, integrity, hard work, and honesty.

Reading is such a great way to help advance character in children. It's also one of the most pleasant activities that the whole family can share. After dinner each night, before the dishes were cleared from the table, Anne Marie led the Ezzo family in a story time. Those times became some of their greatest family memories. All children love stories. Reading, unlike watching a video, forces ns to work, their minds to think, and their hearts

Reading is also a good means of moral education. Children benefit from the examples true life stories provide. They learn right and wrong, good and bad, and the consequences of each. As Bill Bennett says in *The Book of Virtues,* "Nothing in recent years, on television or anywhere else, has improved on a good story that begins 'Once upon a time...'"*

Reading together after dinner did more than add to the Ezzos' minds. It was during times like these that Gary and Anne Marie gave their children what they really needed: a sense of family identity built upon the memories of togetherness. Pick up a book after dinner tonight and start reading as a family.

Allow your kids to plan a family night.

Some people think that having leisure time activities with their children is a luxury. It is not. It's an absolute necessity. Family night helps keep your work and play in perspective.

The Ezzos planned a family night once a week. It was a time when they separated themselves from work and school and came together for family fun. Family night afforded them an informal setting for relaxing with family members who didn't care how their hair looked or what they were wearing.

They eventually added a little twist to their weekly family fun night. Long before they reached their teen years, the children took ownership for every other family night. They set a little budget and

*William J. Bennett, *The Book of Virtues* (New York: Simon & Schuster, 1993), 12.

planned the evening. The family played board and card games, nad indoor picnics, or feasted on pizza and fondue and watched a favorite video classic.

What is the benefit of letting children plan family night? Your children are not just taking ownership of a family night every other week, they are actually taking ownership of your family. It is their investment in the fun portion of other family members' lives. It gives them another good reason to stick around.

Plan family nights. Be intentional about it. Don't allow your children to end up with your leftover time.

Let them participate in building family memories.

If kids can plan family nights, why not let them help plan your next family vacation? Whether it be a short weekend camping trip or a weeklong journey, planning and participating adds a positive memory-building dimension to the experience for your middle-years child. The healthier the memories, the more interdependent your family becomes.

Building memories with your children means more than taking them places and doing fun things with them. It requires that they participate in all aspects of the activity. Some friends of the authors realized this truth many years ago. For years each February they packed up the kids and left cold northern New England to spend two weeks in Florida. Every year, they returned home discouraged by their children's constant complaints and lack of appreciation for all the parents had done.

Then one year someone suggested that they let their kids help plan the next family trip. That included letting them help decide the travel route, make some of the scheduling decisions, and select some of the special events they would attend along the way. It made all the difference in the world. The children became participants in the vacation instead of spectators. And the overall benefit? The work that went into planning and scheduling, the anticipation of seeing those plans realized, and the sense of ownership all helped build lasting memories for the entire family.

If your response to this is, "Yeah, right. Three hundred years ago, maybe," give it a chance. They may surprise you and accept this simple suggestion.

Take walks together.

The Ezzos and Bucknams found that taking walks with their children, one at a time, initiated talks they otherwise would not have had. It gave us insights into their young lives. There is something about a twenty-minute walk that causes people to reflect, open up, and share their hearts. Those moments of reflection often led to very personal and private conversations.

Walking with our children gave them access to us and us access to them. They exposed their inner thoughts, fears, doubts, and hopes. Sometimes they just needed to talk, which meant those walks were good times for us, their parents, just to listen. We knew that our listening served a purpose: It provided a sounding board to help our children sort things out.

Dining, reading, planning, playing, and walking together—this is just a partial list of the activities the Ezzos and Bucknams have enjoyed with their families. Make your own list. See if you can come up with ten options. What are some of your family members' favorite activities? Pick one or two that you can try doing together this week. And do them!

SUMMARY

Our work with parents affords us a greater-than-average opportunity to observe and study the characteristics of healthy and not so healthy families. We have followed a number of children from the high chair through high school. While not every healthy family will exhibit identical characteristics, we have found that they all demonstrate interdependence.

To check the relationship bonds being created in your home, take a careful look at the answers to these questions: What will our family identity be in another three, five, or ten years? Have we cultivated a team spirit in our home? Have we instilled a neighbor-honoring value system in our children's lives? Who else is raising our children?

Family structures can either promote or hinder healthy parent-child relationships, as well as sibling relationships. Work now to develop healthy family roles. In twenty years, you just may find yourself drifting slowly down a river on a wonderful weeklong vacation with your entire clan. And liking it.

BRINGING IT HOME

1. What is the difference between an independent family and an interdependent family?

2. How is the interdependent family model initiated by Mom and Dad in the home?

3. On what basis do teens select peer groups?

4. What are at least three family identity builders that you are ready to practice in your home?

Chapter Ten

The Power of Groupthink

She's ten, with misty blue toenails emerging from the worn hem of her baggy blue jeans. Propping herself on the edge of your bed, she asks once more about the movie.

"Rachel's seen it, and you always say how nice her parents seem. Mom, even Kara's been to it twice. Twice! And she's not even allowed to go to skating parties," says your petite package of impending womanhood, with just a hint of desperation. "Honest, Mom. I am the only one in the entire fourth grade who hasn't been at least once. Except for Ben, of course. But that's just Ben. Mom, how can I live through this year without this movie?"

You've probably noticed by now that your family is not the only influence on your child. During the middle years, peer culture is an ever-growing force steering his or her thoughts and actions. Teachers, coaches, school workers, and other family members all continue to make an impact. Yet none will shape behavior as much as hormones and peers.

The movie? Very possibly your child knows more about her peers' toenails than she does about the story line of this must-see movie. Undoubtedly, she's no more ready to observe intimate love scenes or the terror of life-threatening circumstances than the rest of her group, who one by one managed to wear their mothers down. (And they call this *peer* pressure.)

Where once she valued Mom's opinion above all others, suddenly the collective opinion of her friends—what we refer to as *groupthink*—matters just as much or more. Although socializing with children of the same age is a natural part of growing up, it's not until the middle and early teen years that a child becomes fully aware of what it means to belong to a group of peers. And it is not until this time that parents realize the full impact of peer relationships.

HORMONES, BODY CHANGES, AND PEERS

The mix is unique. Think about it: erupting hormones, some pretty serious body changes, and that ever-present social factor pressing in on your child's world. It should be no surprise that these forces, unleashed in unison, have a profound impact on your preadolescent. Here are two examples.

1. A Growing Interest in the Opposite Sex

When ten-year-old Tracy came in from outside one spring day, she mentioned something so shocking and strange that a chill went down her mother's spine. "Mom, Cindy and I just saw Billy ride past on his bike. I think he's really cute, don't you?"

Mom simply wasn't prepared. How could anything nice be said about a B-O-Y? The boy is cute. Oh, no. Mom envisions a twenty-first century version of spin-the-bottle. Mom—not Tracy—needs to cool off.

What's happening here is perfectly normal. Typically, parents of preteens don't want to hear that their children are starting to feel drawn to the opposite sex. However, this is a reality for your middle-years child. Will you encourage open lines of communication on this topic? Or will your child learn early on that this is not something you care to discuss?

Just yesterday, it seems, the girls thought the boys were "icky." But suddenly, boys are starting to look good to the girls, and vice versa. This is a natural attraction, Mom and Dad. No need for alarm. By *attraction* we are not implying any kind of sexual fantasy. We simply mean that members of the opposite sex are starting to be more appealing.

The girls are looking at the boys, and the boys are looking at the girls. Interestingly, they are also noticing that other girls are looking at boys and that some of the boys are looking at the girls. A new awareness of the opposite sex is taking place. This is a part of the hormonal nudge.

2. *A Greater Sensitivity to Differences between Self and Peers*

During the middle years, both boys and girls begin to notice that the peer group is changing. For the most part, girls change sooner than boys, and they start to compare the changes that are taking place.

This can cause preteens to get very emotional at times. After all, the body changes at its own rate. The child has absolutely no control. That's a frightening thing. It's also terribly frustrating because one of the unwritten rules of preadolescence is that whatever it is the child wants his or her body to do, it refuses to do—and whatever it's not supposed to do, that it does with a vengeance. The preteen is convinced that his body is out to ruin his life.

When this happens, it is important for parents to come alongside and help them see what Mom and Dad's physical structures are like. Perhaps you have a son who has recently returned to school after summer vacation. He sees that many of his peers have shot up five or six inches while he has remained the same height. He is now looking around, thinking, "What's wrong with me?"

Dad, it's your responsibility—and privilege—to talk your son through both the situation and his feelings. It may be appropriate to say, "Well, you take after me, son," or to simply let him know that in time he will grow.

Boys also can be clumsy at this age. Often, their bodies don't grow proportionally. Perhaps his body grows and his head stays small, or his head grows while his body lags behind. Meanwhile the girls are getting prettier. Your son may feel insecure about how they will perceive him. There is a whole new awareness of his physical being.

Mom and Dad, your preteen will need your support as he or she begins to work through these natural comparisons.

AN INDIRECT EFFECT ON THE PARENT-CHILD RELATIONSHIP

Hormones, body changes, interest in the opposite sex, and peer pressure do not occur off on a desert island somewhere. They happen right in your home, and they impact your relationship with your preadolescent.

Let's say you and your family live in Kristin Howard's neighborhood. Recently you've noticed that little Kristin is developing into a lovely young lady. You realize that your son has noticed this as well, so you're not surprised when he tells you that instead of doing his homework he wants to go riding with "the kids" in the neighborhood. He's not going to come right out and say, "I want to go to Kristin's house." But he will resist doing his homework if it interferes with seeing her.

As long as you ignore the heart of the issue, you and your son will have conflict about the homework. Sit down with him (or, better yet, go replace the spark plugs with him) and say, "Now, what really is the issue?" Start opening up the lines of communication so you can enter into a deep and meaningful conversation.

The bottom line is this: Hormones may affect the body, but they do not affect the heart. The values you place in her heart—not the hormones—will drive your child. Make sure those values are there. Make sure that you're working on instilling that higher standard in your child. Remember to teach her about good, better, and best. Help your preteen learn to think morally on her own. These are the things that will ultimately bring harmony to your family and your child to moral maturity.

WHAT DOES THE GROUP THINK?

Your middle-years child is now moving from a gentle awakening to a full awareness of the significance of his group's opinion. Much of this change is hormone-activated. This is what brings about peer relationships and thus peer pressure. Not only does the child want to know what the group thinks, he wants to know what the group thinks of him.

It is a natural human tendency to seek social approval. Think back to when you were a preteen. Remember how much you wanted to be a part of the group and how wonderful it felt when they included you? Today you probably feel many of those same feelings about your adult peer groups. You want to be accepted. Your child feels the same way.

These feelings are normal, but they can also be dangerous. A child's sense of social belonging is often tied to how well he or she meets peer group standards and expectations. As a result, preteens quickly learn that if they deviate even slightly from the group's standards, they may be ridiculed or even rejected. Thus, peer pressure brings about the need to conform.

To most of us, the words *peer pressure* have a negative connotation. Yet, in and of itself, peer pressure is not evil. It is simply a socializing force that challenges a person's thinking and behavior. Peer pressure on middle-years children becomes negative only when the peer group's values oppose those of the parents.

To ensure peer acceptance under such conditions, the middle-years child learns that he must accept the group's interests and values. He cannot afford to be different because that would jeopardize his status within the group. To demonstrate his allegiance, he acts out his new association and conforms to the group's identity. This might manifest itself in choice of hairstyle, clothes, music, and the use of slang or foul language.

So you can see why it's so important that your child have the right friends. Your preteen must assess and decide which is more significant—the approval of his peers or his parents—or he must find a happy medium.

A GROWING INTEREST IN THE GROUP

Think back to when your child was between the ages of two and four. You may recall that at that time, he or she didn't really care about the group. The only time small children will stay with the group is when the older kids in it show attention to them. If the older kids stop playing with the younger ones, the little ones will go off to the toy room and find something else to do. The group is just not interesting enough to keep their attention.

Between the ages of four and eight, children become more interested in the group. It now has momentary significance to them. These kids may play football, even if they don't like the game, simply because they like the group. There's a growing interest in the power of being associated with a group, though often that interest is only temporary.

When a child is in the eight-to-nineteen age range, the group takes on an even greater significance. The group's opinion now means more than ever. If all of the nine-year-old girls in your daughter's class are wearing green and your daughter is not, that's going to mean something to her. If she is a Brownie or a Bluebird and all the other girls are wearing a uniform, it will be vital to her that she wear one as well. If all the other boys are wearing their baseball hats to school, your son will probably want to as well.

Wearing green or a cap is pretty benign. Such actions are not hurting anyone or compromising any values. But morally neutral peer pressure can quickly turn ugly.

In the years ahead, your child is going to be pulled in many different moral directions. The world is filled with a wide variety of value systems, and for the first time he or she will be faced with these alternatives. During this time you must protect your child from negative peer pressure while reinforcing your family values.

COMBATING NEGATIVE PEER PRESSURE

It is the conflict in values, not the power of peer pressure itself, that tears adolescents from their parents. The closer the values between parents and child, the stronger the family allegiance, and the less likely the child will be to drift away from Mom and Dad during the teen years.

Please understand that a healthy family has not eliminated normal peer pressure as much as it has developed healthy ways to deal with it. This is why it is wrong to cite peer pressure as the primary cause of drug use, crime, rebellion, sexual promiscuity, and the general breakdown of the family. Fundamentally, the problem is a matter of incompatible values.

Thankfully, there are things you can do to protect your children from negative peer pressure while reinforcing your values. In order for this to happen, you must take advantage of three important resources:

- the power of family identity;
- the power of community;
- the power of age-related wisdom.

THE POWER OF FAMILY IDENTITY

Though we covered this at length in the previous chapter, we'd like to repeat just one idea as it relates to peer pressure: The peer pressure your child feels will be only as strong as your family identity is weak.

THE POWER OF COMMUNITY

Community can mean many things to many people. We use it to refer to a group of families sharing common interests, values, and a significant commitment to an ideal for the mutual benefit of the individual and the collective membership. In other words, to quote the Three Musketeers, "All for one and one for all!"

Why is it important to have a community? Because a community does something that nothing else can: It establishes a sense of "we-ness" in the group that encourages members to work toward a common good. As we've seen in our large cities, where virtually everyone is unknown to everyone else, the absence of we-ness causes accountability to disappear—and with it, common morality. That will always be to your children's detriment. Where there is no common standard to strive for, there will be limited expectations of your children.

Connecting with a Moral Community

Since members of your community are going to teach your children (directly or indirectly), it is vital that you surround yourself with people who share your morals and values. In a moral community, you will find people who are striving to live out respect and honor and to instill in their children a moral awareness and consideration of others. These are the people who can provide a support group for you, Mom and Dad.

Your child will find his or her friends in your community. You want those friends to be moral kids—kids whose moms and dads are working to instill values in their hearts just as you are with your child. A like-minded moral community is vital.

During these middle years, your son or daughter's interests will broaden; attachment to friends will become more meaningful. He or she is becoming morally and relationally emancipated and self-reliant. That is why the moral community to which you and your child belong will either be a friend or foe to your family values. Children do better when the community they grow up in reinforces the values the parents are trying to instill.

Remember, the greater the disparity between the values of your family and your community (from which you and your child both will draw peers), the greater the source of conflict within the home. The opposite is also true: Shared values between community and home result in positive peer pressure on your child.

This truth is illustrated by the story of a young girl we know whose orthodontist decided she needed to wear headgear. Though he strongly recommended that she wear the headgear twenty-four hours a day, he said to her, "I realize, though, that you probably can't wear it at school because the kids might laugh at you."

"Oh, no," the girl told him. "Not at my school. The kids won't laugh at me there." This child felt secure in her community. She knew she would not be ridiculed. This gave her the strength she needed to help her do what she knew was best—wear the headgear at all times.

How would your child respond in this situation? Would the children in his or her circle of friends say, "Do what's right. Wear the headgear"? Or would they say, "Don't listen to your mom and dad. You look like a loser"? It is time to take a look at who is in your family's community.

At this point, we must make one important clarification. By urging you to surround your family with people who share your morals and values, we are not suggesting that you should isolate your children from the rest of the world. That, in our opinion, is going too far. However, we do want to insulate our children from corruptive influences.

When the Ezzos lived in New England years ago, every floor, ceiling, and outside wall was insulated. They insulated their home because they did not want the elements to disturb the healthy environment they were providing for their children. That insulation did not keep every element out. It slowed the process of cold coming into the house, but it did not keep the wind from rushing in when the door was opened. It was also true that they could not stay in the house all the time. It was necessary and important for them to go out into the world around them. The insulated house did, however, give them a place where they could find safety and warmth and be refreshed.

By the same token, a moral community insulates your child against the elements of the world. Through association with like-minded peers, your children will see family standards reinforced by others who share the same values. The strength they draw from moral peers is the very thing that makes it possible for you as parents to let them participate in Little League or a community soccer league. The support of a moral community allows our families to be a blessing to others because we know that the moral strength we draw from our like-minded community allows us to present something very beautiful to the world.

THE POWER OF AGE-RELATED WISDOM

Sociologists say that America will have a shortfall of qualified laborers in twenty years. As baby boomers begin to retire, there will not be enough new workers around to fill the void. Solution? Go back and hire some of those aged baby boomers and utilize that good old-fashioned wisdom that only life experience can bring.

In ancient Israel, town elders sat at the gate deciding matters of importance. When men and women living in those times needed counsel on the sale of property, help with a business investment, or wisdom on how to deal with a troublesome child, they knew where to go. They went to the city gate, the place of the elders.

Today, we still need counsel in all these areas. Sadly, though, we have lost respect for the "aged ones" who could guide us so wisely. Think about it. Who are the elders at your gate?

Having a moral community is important. But we're going to take this idea one step further and tell you that not only do you need a community that includes peers, you also need a community that includes elders. Is this an old-fashioned idea? You bet it is. And one in need of resurgence.

Think for a moment about the people who are in your family's community. Within that mix, who are the parents who have gone before you? Where do you get your wisdom: from the media, from public opinion—or from those who have gone before you successfully? Who are the elders in your community?

Not only is it good for you, Mom and Dad, to have this resource, it is also comforting for your child to know that Mom and Dad have someone older and wiser they go to for advice. As you seek the wisdom of elders, you are setting a silent example. Your child sees that you understand that you need wisdom from an elder who knows what you are going through. As a result, he or she will be more inclined to come to you than to peers for wisdom when the need for guidance arises.

It may not immediately be apparent who your elders are. You may have to look around. Where do you begin? Start by considering your grandparents and even your parents. How can you involve them in your lives?

Your parents or grandparents may not be living or may not be in your area. However, it is likely that *someone's* grandparents live in your community. Invite them in. Tell them what you're doing. Embrace them and their wisdom. Ask for their advice.

SUMMARY

The middle years are the time when physiological changes begin to nudge children to an awareness of themselves and of the opposite sex. This spawns a new era of significant peer relationships. New social stresses are placed on the child, and as a result, on the parent-child relationship.

This has always been so and will continue to be as long as man lives on this earth. Parents do make the difference when it comes to healthy parent-preteen and parent-teen relationships because moms and dads make choices every day. How obedient are you to the moral precepts that you require—every day? Have you been working on your family identity—every day? Who is in your family's community—every day? You must evaluate your reponses to these questions honestly because the answers will have a tremendous impact on your family's future.

BRINGING IT HOME

1. When does peer pressure become negative?

2. What makes middle-years children and teens more vulner-able to peer pressure?

3. Why is community important to the successful rearing of children?

4. In addition to a healthy family identity, why is a moral community necessary?

5. Who are the elders in your family's community?

Chapter Eleven

Tips for Healthy Communication

"Mom," says your ten-year-old, "Joey offered me a joint at the bus stop today. He hid it when he saw the bus driver. He told me he'd let me try some after school tomorrow. I'm scared, Mom. What should I do?"

Your mind races. Suddenly you see yourself at the wheel of that bus, bearing down on Joey. *Joey, Joey, Joey.* It becomes your silent mantra of death. Joey's gotta go. You want him off this planet.

But Joey's just a microcosm of the problem. The world is swarming with Joeys—and worse. Your challenge, and opportunity, stands before you now in this priceless moment of open, trusting communication.

Creating and maintaining a climate of trust in which your kids feel secure in communicating openly and honestly with you must be a high priority as you parent your middle-years children.

How are your preteen's communication skills developing? As family educators, we have observed that how a child communicates during the middle years is usually how he or she will communicate in adulthood. You may think that you already understand your child's communication style. But, as we have already seen, things tend to change dramatically during the middle years.

Billy talked excessively from first through third grade. But he became more reserved during the middle years as he began to gain greater self-control in both speech and conduct. Another example of this phenomenon is Lindsey, who was shy in early childhood but gained the confidence to be a great communicator during the middle years.

Good communication skills do not ensure family harmony. Nor are communication skills a substitute for values. What holds families together is moral unity. Take for example the scene with Joey. If there hadn't been trust and openness in that family, that ten-year-old never would never have told his mother about what Joey had done. You don't want your child to think, *I could never tell Mom and Dad about that.* You want to be the elder at your child's gate.

Without a common moral foundation, Mom and Dad have no genuine power to lead their children. There is no substitute for moral intimacy among family members. That's why we believe good speaking and listening skills are important parts of, but not a substitute for, healthy relationships.

You probably know of great communicators who have little, if any, relationship with their kids. Knowing how to communicate with your spouse and kids is certainly important. But it is more important that you first learn to love and live with your family. Unconditional love is the vehicle used to develop this bond.

KEYS TO HEALTHY COMMUNICATION

One of the best ways we can encourage our middle-years is through healthy, proactive communication. Good communication, that rests on a common moral foundation can prevent more conflicts than corrections can ever solve.

Preadolescents and teens communicate their feelings much more readily than do younger children, possibly because their vocabulary is more extensive. The words needed to reflect abstract feelings are now present, making meaningful conversations possible. Take advantage of this. Now is the time to establish communication patterns that will help you avoid and work through conflict. You must learn how to talk so your kids will listen and how to listen so your kids will talk.

Here are some tips that will help.

1. Accentuate the positive.

We are concerned that parents typically spend more time and energy suppressing bad behavior than elevating good behavior in their children. While correction is a primary component of the training process, we must also retrain ourselves to communicate the positive. This will take self-discipline, but the efforts will pay great dividends.

When communicating with your children, attempt to speak as often as possible in the positive. If there is something you don't want your child to do, then communicate your desire for restraint by speaking positively about what you want done.

165

Instead of this:	Consider this:
"Don't spill your cereal."	"See how carefully you can carry your cereal bowl."
"Don't get out of bed."	"Obey Mommy and stay in bed."
"Don't hit your sister."	"You need to show kindness to your sister."
"Don't talk so much."	"You need to learn to become a good listener."
"Don't chew with your mouth open."	"Chew quietly with your mouth closed."
"Don't leave a mess for everyone else to clean up."	"Be responsible and clean up after yourself."

With young children there will be plenty of justifiable "don'ts." "Don't touch the knives." "Don't play with the stereo." "Don't hit the dog." Such prohibitions are appropriate with young children. But the middle-years child is in need of positive direction. He will not get it unless you change the way you communicate your prohibitions. The no you are trying to communicate can be expressed as a yes. Consider the transfer from negative to positive speech another middle-years transition—for you.

Talk Times

2. *Create opportunities to talk and listen.*

Children need to have access to Mom and Dad. It is important for your kids to know that you are open to what they have to say and that you will understand. If your middle-years children don't have the option of coming to you, they will begin to take things into their own hands. They will come up with their own solutions for problems, often making choices that are not in their best interests.

At this point in your child's life, this may not seem like a critical issue. You may think your child knows he or she can come and talk to you. You take the fact that your preteen rarely does so as a sign that at this time, he or she has no real need for meaningful conversations.

Do not make the mistake of assuming there is no need. Your child must have deep, meaningful conversations with you. He or she may not be aware of the need, but it is there. Even when children realize they need to talk to Mom and Dad, they may not know how to make it happen.

You must create the opportunity for healthy talk and healthy listening. This may take some planning on your part. If you are extremely busy, you may need to schedule some time to sit down and talk. This may be especially difficult if you are not a talker. Perhaps you and your spouse can go for hours or days with minimal conversation. Your relationship is fine; you just aren't big talkers. Yet you may have a child who is a talker. He or she will need even more conversation than a child who is not.

Even quiet children must learn to have deep conversations. It is likely that one day in the future your child will choose to be married. Your success at engaging in family conversation today will dramatically impact his or her relationship with your future son- or daughter-in-law.

This will become increasingly important as your child approaches the teen years. If he or she is now eight or nine years old, there will be less of a need than there will be at ten or twelve. However, even then you are still preparing for adolescence. Do not wait until the teen years are upon you to begin developing your communication skills.

Consider these conversation scenarios:

1. Father Talk Times

It is vitally important that dads carve out time in which they can talk to their sons and daughters privately. This can be done through everyday activities: Go shopping together, throw a football, take walks, or go out to breakfast. No matter what the activity, these times together will provide great opportunities for conversation and bonding. Even if you don't talk about anything heavy, you'll be amazed at the subtle improvements in the way your child relates to you.

2. Mother Talk Times

Mothers often feel as though they do a lot of talking with their kids, particularly during the early years. However, communication is going to look dramatically different during the middle years. Moms now must allow their kids to do more of the talking, while they develop the skill of listening.

If you have been a talkative mom, you'll find yourself being stretched during these years as you must listen more. If you have in the past been fairly quiet, you may have to learn to talk more. Or perhaps you're simply not very comfortable with the idea of having more equal conversations with your child. Strive for meaningful conversations with your child, Mom.

3. Father-Mother Talk Time

Kids need talk times that involve both Mom and Dad. As you move toward the teen years, this needs to happen on a regular basis. In the Ezzo home, whenever one child stayed over at a friend's house for the weekend, Gary and Anne Marie attempted to have some special time with the sibling left at home. As a trio, they would do something out of the ordinary. This situation provided a perfect opportunity to talk, listen, and find out what was going on in the life of this particular child.

Don't wait until problems arise before saying, "The three of us are going to talk." That will put your child on the defensive. When these talk times happen on a regular basis, however, you will be able to use them as a conversation tool when serious talks do need to occur. Your child will feel comfortable talking with Mom and Dad when it matters most.

4. Family Talk Times

In chapter 10 we talked about groupthink. Now we're talking about "family think." Your middle-years child needs to know what your family thinks. You need to have times when you're all together as a family—not in front of the TV.

Mealtimes may now provide this opportunity for you. But in just a few years, this will probably occur most often at bedtime. Once your child gets his or her driver's license, it will be harder to find times when all family members are home at the same time.

5. Husband-Wife Talk Times

In *Childwise*, we introduced a practice called "couch time." This is a regular time, ten to fifteen minutes or so, in which Mom and Dad sit together and talk to each other. They must do this while the child is awake, since the whole point is to demonstrate to her the strength of your marriage. The child may play quietly in the same room, but may not interrupt. Just sit there and talk about your day. You may find that couch time does as much to solidify your marriage as it does to make your child feel her world is secure.

3. Be sensitive to the sorting process.

As we have already discovered, your middle-years child is going through a number of transitions—moral, biological, and relational. Sometimes new challenges in life are not easily harmonized with the old, well-worn beliefs that have guided the child thus far. Sorting out the various issues of life is one of the primary tasks to be tackled in pre- and early adolescence. Often middle-years children talk at a surface level, but confusion lurks at a deeper one. This is where gentle conversational probing comes in.

Sissy's Story

Although she didn't see her same-age cousins often, eleven-year-old Sissy was always glad when they went home. Her mother sensed this attitude and began to probe.

"Sissy," Mom said, "every time you know your cousins are coming to visit you're excited. But once they get here, you seem agitated."

"Oh, Mom. Sarah and Kim are so bossy when they come over. I always have to do what they want."

"Well, you know, honey, they are our guests. We want to be hospitable, and they only come for the weekend."

"But it bothers me."

"I know, sweetie. But sometimes people come into our live. teach us things, like how to be kind to people who bother us."

At this point, Sissy's surface message was about her bossy cousins. Mom attempted to work this issue through with her child, but she sensed that something more was going on in Sissy's heart. She also realized that Sissy herself might not understand her own feelings.

"Sissy, do you remember when you were a little girl? I used to hold you on my lap, and we would talk. Would you let me hold you now?"

Sissy climbed into Mom's lap.

"Honey," Mom said, "is something else bothering you?"

"I don't know."

"But you do understand how sometimes even irritating people help shape us into better human beings?"

"I know, Mom, but they always want to hang around with Brian and Daddy. I'm just in the way."

So that was it. Mom gave her daughter a squeeze. "No, honey, you're not in the way. But you have to remember, Sarah and Kim don't have an older brother or a dad living in the house. One of the reasons they like to come here is because they get to share Daddy and Brian with us."

"That's what I don't like about them coming. They're making Brian and Daddy love them more than me."

"Oh, honey. No one can replace you. You belong to Daddy and Brian in a way your cousins never could. You will always receive their special love. No one wants to take that away from you. And even if they wanted to, it wouldn't be possible."

story, it was Mom's sensitivity that was able to
 ep fear. It is sometimes difficult for a middle-
 beyond his or her own fears. In Sissy's case, her
fear or disp... ent kept her from understanding her cousins'
tremendous need for male attention. Mom helped put all this into
perspective for her.

Finding their way into your preteen's rapidly expanding world
are new relationships, emotions, attitudes, experiences, and sensations. They come in twisted and tangled and need to be sorted out.
Do you remember the uniformed gate agents who greet arriving
passengers and help them on their journey? During the middle-
years phase of growth and development, your child will need your
help in sorting life out. He or she will emerge from childhood into
a world that sometimes does not make sense.

Listen for unspoken messages like these. Pay attention to signals your child is sending through body language, facial expression,
tone of voice, and an overall sense of urgency. These nonverbal cues
will give you invaluable insights to the message your child is trying
to communicate and the issues of life he or she is facing.

4. Guard your tongue and tone.

One day, twelve-year-old Barry came home from school with great
news: The teacher had selected him to be first-chair trombone in his
seventh-grade band class. That evening when his dad came home from
work, Barry ran into the kitchen and shouted, "Guess what, Dad! I
made first chair!" Overcome with enthusiasm, he let his imagination
soar and cried out, "I'm going to be a musician when I grow up!"

What was Dad to think? He'd just come home from a frustrating day at work. Bills were due. More month than money. The lawn needed mowing. "Not if you want to make any money, you're not," he said.

Barry's face fell. He hung his head and turned away. As his father watched him retreat from the living room, he realized he had made a grave error. His son had tried to share something with him that was of great importance to him. In his rush to protect his child, Dad had stolen the joy from his son's heart. In that moment, Barry did not need an analytical assessment of his career aspirations. He wanted his dad to enter into his excitement.

Remember these two rules of thumb when responding to your preteen.

- Measure your response against the excitement on his or her face:
- Think before you speak.

The Ezzos wish someone had shared this principle with them when they were young parents. Gary remembers the morning their youngest daughter, Jennifer, came running into the house with an enormous pinecone. In her desire to share this discovery, she set it on the kitchen table and exclaimed: "Dad, look at it!" Her entire face was glowing with excitement, and she wanted to share that feeling with her daddy.

In that moment, as Gary tells it, he failed. What Jennifer saw was a beautiful treasure. What he saw was a mess. Disturbed, he turned to her and said, "Jennifer, get that thing off the table. It's full of ants and sand and goo!"

Those words destroyed a special moment in the life of a little girl. As he watched the joy and excitement drain from her face, he asked himself, "Why? Why that tone? Why those words?"

When your child comes to you with excitement and joy written on his or her face, make sure you guard your tongue and tone. If we fail our kids in their moments of discovery, we potentially lose more than the moment: We lose our children's trust. Maybe they will stop coming to us altogether.

5. *Show your child you know the feeling.*

At nine, Laura had already shown signs of true artistic ability. Drawing was one of her favorite activities, and it made her feel good when others acknowledged her talent. When she entered a school-wide poster contest, Laura became extremely excited. She worked hard on her entry for weeks and hoped she would win first prize.

Instead, she placed third. Her disappointment was increased by the fact that top honors went to her best friend. Not only did Laura feel a sense of loss, she struggled with feelings of resentment and jealousy.

Laura's mother, Sandra, knew how Laura felt. She remembered a time in junior high when she had lost the leading role in her school play to her friend. By sharing that story and her own emotions with her daughter, Sandra was able to help her through a difficult experience. She helped Laura come to terms with her feelings and to even find a sense of accomplishment in the fact that her work had been honored. Best of all, Laura was assured that Mom knew what she was going through.

Don't wait for a moment of crisis to occur. You can routinely tell your child stories about your life. Make the stories a regular part of your relationship with your children. That way, when trials occur, your son or daughter can think, "Something like this happened to Mom, too" or "Daddy understands what I'm going through."

During the middle years, your child is experiencing different, greater, and more complex emotions than ever before. Understandably, many kids lack confidence and develop feelings of inadequacy when they find themselves in new situations. Sometimes they feel emotionally isolated because they think (just as you did when you were their age) that Mom and Dad could never understand what they are facing.

Of course that is not true. Although we grew up in a different time and place, the emotions we experienced in our youth were just as real as the ones our kids feel today. Do your kids know that? You don't want to try to be their buddy, protesting that you're just like them. But you do want them to know you have a fully functioning set of emotions and that you can at least relate to what they're going through.

Most powerful of all are the stories about you, Mom and Dad, in your childhood. One story in particular helped the Ezzo children understand that their dad fully understood the feeling of disappointment.

When Gary was a child, he lived to fish. He loved to hit a stream or a lake for the day, and he enjoyed himself even more when he could fish somewhere guaranteed to give him a good day's catch. That is why he was excited to receive Mr. and Mrs. Wadsworth's invitation to join them the weekend they opened their cottage on White Birch Lake. It was bluegill heaven—teeming with fish ready to hit anything offered as bait.

The Wadsworths told Gary's parents they would call early on Saturday morning to confirm the trip. If they did not call, it meant they would go some other time. All week Gary dreamed about the upcoming weekend. On Saturday morning at 8:00 the phone rang. Smiling, Gary's mother picked up the phone.

"Hi," the man's voice said. "It's us. Just calling to tell you to get the boy ready, we're going. We'll be by in ten minutes."

"Okay," Gary's mom said, "he'll be ready."

In ninety seconds flat Gary gathered his pole, worms, and tackle box, and dashed to the end of the driveway. There he stood, looking up the road, anticipating seeing the Wadsworths' silver, 1950 Plymouth headed his way.

He waited. Five minutes. Ten minutes. Fifteen. He reminded himself about being patient. Older people (those over forty) were sometimes slow and forgetful, he told himself. They had probably just forgotten a few things. After another twenty minutes, he began to wonder if something had happened. The Wadsworths only lived down the street.

Gary went into the house to ask his mom to call. Maybe there had been some confusion. Maybe he was to meet them at their house. What if they were waiting for him? Even worse, what if they had gone without him? His mom dialed the phone. Gary went back to the curb.

"Henry, this is Anna Ezzo," his mom said. "Gary's been waiting for you out front ever since you called. Will you be coming by shortly?"

"Anna," Mr. Wadsworth said, "there must be a mistake. We never called you this morning. Something came up at the last minute, and we're not going up to the lake."

Gary's mother realized it had all been an amazing coincidence. The first call had been a wrong number. Whoever called had just happened to say enough right things to make her think it was Mr. Wadsworth.

Today, Gary can still see in his mind's eye his mother walking down the driveway. He knew by looking at her face that he wasn't going. She told him what had happened and explained that he wouldn't be going to the lake after all. All the hopes a little boy could muster were dashed. In that moment, he knew what disappointment was. Years later, when his own children were facing similar disappointments, Gary could relate.

On a sheet of paper, list what you consider to be the most common human emotions. Write down things like disappointment, joy, anger, hurt, rejection, and any others you think of. Then think back to your own childhood. Think of stories from your past that illustrate how you experienced these emotions. Share one of these stories with your child in the coming week.

In doing so, you will instill in your child a confidence that Mom and Dad can relate—and that he or she can relate to you. This confidence will keep your middle-years child turning to you in the times of emotional turmoil that lie ahead.

SUMMARY

One of the best ways for us to encourage our preteens is through healthy, proactive communication. Stress the *dos* over the *don'ts*. Create opportunities to talk and listen. Listen for the deeper meaning of what your child tells you. Be careful what you say and how you say it. And let your child know you understand the feelings he or she is going through.

If your preadolescent can come to Mom and Dad with all his questions and hurts, he won't need to look for other sounding boards.

BRINGING IT HOME

1. Listen to how you talk to your middle-years child. Do you tend to speak negatively? The next time you catch yourself saying *don't,* correct yourself and make it *do.*

2. When is your family usually all together? If it's only when the TV is on, next time turn it off and play a talk game instead. Go around the room answering a question like: "What would you want people to say about you at your funeral?"

3. Think back to a time when what you said or how you said it hurt your child's feelings. Is there a hurt left unresolved? Remember, don't be afraid to apologize to your children.

4. Why should you tell your children your life stories?

FATHERS

AND

MOTHERS

Chapter Twelve

A Word to Dad

The father of a great football player was being interviewed on TV. The son had just broken another all-time NFL record. When the interviewer asked the player's father what he thought of his son, he said something unforgettable.

He said his son would never be as good as the great Jim Brown.

Never mind that the son had surpassed Brown's records. Never mind that he was arguably the greatest player ever to play the game. Never mind that no one was even close to his career yardage and scoring totals. To his father, this future Hall-of-Famer was a failure.

There is nothing more powerful in the life of a child than his father. A father who parents with care gives his child a healthy, stable sense of confidence. A father who does it wrong has the power to break his child's spirit.

This is a chapter for fathers: fathers of sons and fathers of daughters. We'd like to talk about how you can be the father your children so desperately need.

A DAD WORTHY OF TRUST

"Daddy, will you catch me?" Before you can answer, your toddler throws herself off the three-foot-high stone wall. She knew you would be there.

Children are naturally trusting. Especially in the early years, they believe everything their parents say. Make believe you pinch off her nose and she searches your hand to find it. Pretend to put it back and she sighs with relief.

But during the middle years, your children begin transitioning from absolute trust to reasoned trust. Their intellectual capacities have increased to the point that they understand that a leap from the retaining wall would really hurt if everything didn't go just right. If they decided to do it at all, it would only be if they were perfectly certain you would catch them. Even then, they might just decide to crawl down another way.

Mom and Dad, your middle-years child doesn't trust you "just because" anymore. You can earn or lose his trust based on how well you keep faith with him. It's an invisible process, but it's there just the same. He will trust you to the degree that you prove yourself trustworthy. There is no time in your parenting to grow lax and assume your believability does not matter. It always will.

Life is full of uncertainty. Adults know this all too well. But your preadolescent is discovering it perhaps for the first time. His body is changing; his friendships are changing; his understanding is changing; and his interests are changing. Everything seems to be unstable. The last thing your middle-years child needs is instability at home. You, Dad, are the key to this.

Are you characterized more by promises kept or broken? Are

you emotionally available to your child? Are you *physically* present? Are you involved in her life and her projects? Do you speak gently to her? Patiently?

Do you realize that you are your child's hero? The impact of a father—that strong protector guarding him since he can remember—cannot be overemphasized. But hero status is a fragile thing. Enough harsh words, enough disinterest, enough promises broken, and your child will find other heroes. That place in your child's heart is yours to lose.

Children learn through disappointment that the problem with trusting people is that they are not always trustworthy. The degree to which trust is violated determines whether she ultimately views relationships with suspicion and doubt or with confidence and hope. Give your middle-years child boundless faith in your love and acceptance, Dad. Reassure her of your availability to help her in the critical areas of living.

"Daddy, will you catch me?" Build a relationship now which says, "Count on it."

FAMILY: SOMETHING GREATER THAN ME

Trust is not an emotion. It is confidence in a person, place, or thing. We step into an elevator because we believe the machinery is capable of supporting the weight. Every time we drive over a bridge, we demonstrate our trust in the security of the city's building codes. We go into surgery only after being assured of the skill of the surgeon.

In the same way, children trust their parents for many things. Because we provide them with food, clothing, and shelter, they learn to trust us for their physical well-being. They also learn to trust our judgment: "The stove is hot. Stay away." "The wind is too strong. You'll lose your kite." And they learn to trust our experience: "Milk spoils when it isn't refrigerated." "Black ice is dangerous to walk on."

Perhaps the greatest role trust plays in parenting is in connecting our souls to those of our children. Dads, take this to heart: *The more trust your children have in you, the stronger the relationship.* The strength of the father/child relationship can be seen in how much they trust you.

Trust is the be-all and end-all of fatherhood. Without it, you can never experience intimacy, the soul of human relationships, with your children.* Does your middle-years child trust you to provide her only with sustenance, facts, and experience? Or does the trust extend to a greater degree: Does she trust you as a person?

Trust is the bridge that links a child's need to know that he is loved with the feeling of *being* loved. Trust takes his need to know that he belongs and connects it with a sense of belonging. His need to be accepted is joined, by trust, to the knowledge that he truly is accepted. This is where we fathers come in. Dads are bridge builders. The trust we earn with our children links them to the family. Pity the child who has no one building bridges for him.

Research indicates that adolescents who feel connected to their parents and siblings are less likely than their peers to suffer from emotional distress, experience suicidal thoughts and behaviors, exhibit violent behavior, smoke cigarettes, drink alcohol, or use

---

* The word *intimacy* has come to carry sexual connotations. Of course we do not mean this. The intimacy we are talking about here is an intensely familiar closeness, a deep understanding of another's true self.

drugs. They perform better in school and enjoy deeper relationships.

This sense of connection occurs when each member of the family understands and accepts that he is part of something bigger than himself—his family. Before this can happen, there must be trust between family members. Obviously, middle-years children and teens who do not trust their parents cannot be intimately connected to them. On the other hand, if your child trusts you fully, his peers will not shape his future—you will.

Here are some ideas to help you build this kind of trust with your middle-years child.

Cultivate Affection between Siblings

Tom doesn't go to Billy's T-ball game because nobody he knows will be there—and besides, that's kid stuff. Mary interrupts her little sister whenever she pleases because the brat never talks about anything important anyway.

Too often, age differences are used as excuses for an absence of genuine concern between siblings. This generates resentment between siblings and pulls at the core of your family. If you want to build a trusting relationship with your middle-years child, start by encouraging attitudes that lead to a strong sense of family loyalty.

Family members must exhibit a sincere devotion to one another. This devotion results in relationships that are based on trust and acceptance of each family member as a valued individual, as well as loyalty to the family as a unit. These virtues of trust and loyalty are seen not just in family members' feelings and attitudes, but also in their actions.

You, Dad, need to take the lead in this. Go to as many of your children's games, recitals, and plays as you possibly can attend—for all your children. Urge (perhaps even require) siblings not only to attend these with you, but also to encourage and praise each other. You have more power over the harmony in your home than you may realize. Cultivate sibling affection.

Build Family Identity

The best thing you can do to generate trust as a father is to take the lead in cultivating family identity in your home. If you have come straight to this chapter, Dad, hoping for ideas about what you can do for your family, we urge you to go back and read chapter 9. Even more information can be found in our previous book, *On Becoming Childwise*. However, a little review is in order here.

First, pay attention to your marriage. Make it a beautiful thing, and many parenting problems will solve themselves. A stable marriage is a sure foundation for children because great marriages make for great parents. Demonstrate an ongoing love for your wife. Practice couch time every day. Maintain a regular date night.

Too many of us know how deeply unsettling it is to perceive (on some level, at least) that Mom and Dad aren't happy together. The child believes that at any moment that most fundamental of relationships could disintegrate, dropping him into free fall. No wonder so many children are insecure and act out in bizarre ways. Your children need to see you in love with your wife.

Second, verbalize your commitment to the family whenever appropriate. "I'm so lucky to be part of this fantastic family!" "I'd rather be here with you guys than anywhere else I can think of." A father holds so much power over his family's sense of well-being, but he rarely realizes it. A father's satisfaction and joy with his family will shoot morale through the ceiling.

Understand Your Child's Private World

To find out what is going on with your middle-years child, you need access to her private world. Every person lives in three worlds—public, personal, and private. The public world includes much of the time we spend away from home (e.g., work and social activities) and allows us to keep relationships at a safe distance. Our personal world includes time spent with friends and relatives. In such settings, we are more relaxed and vulnerable.

But it is in our private world that we can be bold one moment and fearful the next. It is a place of intimate thoughts, secret fears, and grand dreams. No one can visit our private world without an invitation. Your middle-years child has a constantly changing private world. Fathers need to be particularly sensitive to this world.

There is an interesting childhood phenomenon we call the "open window." Parents who are too busy may miss it completely. An open window is a moment when your child invites you into his private world. It might happen when you're on a walk with him or putting him to bed or sitting with him in front of a blazing fire. Unexpectedly, children open up the window of their heart and invite you in.

On one occasion, Gary Ezzo was putting Amy, his then five-year-old daughter, to bed. He was gently stroking her hair and asking how school had gone. Suddenly she asked, "Daddy, do you think I'm pretty? Do you think anyone else thinks I'm pretty?" At that moment, she was taking a risk with her dad. She was leaving herself terribly vulnerable, trusting him with the treasures of her heart.

Dad, if your child favors you with moments like this from time to time, you can know you're doing something right. Tickets to a child's private world are not given out cheaply. Remember, trust is the measuring stick for determining the strength of your relationship with your child. When your child is willing to share the issues of his heart, seize the moment. Accept the invitation. But tread lightly. Listen with your heart as well as your head. Guard your tongue and tone.

Though there are no guarantees in parenting, this statement comes close to being an exception: If you prove your trustworthiness during the open-window moments of the middle years, your child will come to you when he is facing life's challenges in the teen years. He will not forget how you treated him when he made himself vulnerable to you.

Give Your Child the Freedom to Fail

Victory, it is said, has a hundred fathers, but defeat is an orphan. Giving anyone, least of all our own children, the freedom to fail sounds almost un-American. In our country, we love winning. Defeat is unacceptable. Win and you're a hero; lose and you're a goat.

It is a crippling thing for a child not to have the freedom to fail in front of Dad. If you hoard your approval and give it out only when your child does something remarkable, you are sending a terrible message. You are saying your love is based solely on something no child can ever live up to—a lifetime of sustained perfection. Anything short of that just doesn't rate.

Some fathers actually believe that by withholding their praise, they are causing their children to push themselves to their capacity. They might even point to how it appears to be working. But what they've done is create a wretched child desperately clawing for his father's approval. The tragedy is that such fathers are usually sitting around waiting for their children to thank them.

Believe it or not, a child who receives her father's approval *will* strive for excellence. She won't do it to gain anyone's affections, but because she is *unafraid to risk failure*. She knows that her standing in her father's eyes is secure—that it does not rise and fall with the outcomes of her own efforts.

Encourage your middle-years child to take chances and try new things. But be sure he knows your love for him doesn't change whether he takes chances or not—or whether he succeeds or not. Tell him: "Anything worth doing well is worth doing terribly for a time." Reassure him that failure is acceptable, as long as he makes an honest effort. Show that you view his failures as the first steps to success.

A father's wrong attitude toward failure can backfire. It can actually prevent his child from stretching to his full potential. Imagine a child who is afraid to fail in front of his father because he knows Dad will draw back from him if he does. "Dad won't love me as much if I blow it." This child will take one of two paths. Either he will whip himself up to try to reach a level of excellence that will finally earn his father's full approval, or he will live well below his potential and never attempt much at all. After all, if the best I can do doesn't please him, why try? The child of a disapproving father simply cannot win.

Such a child fails if he tries the first approach because, as we saw with the football player at the beginning of the chapter, Dad keeps moving the end zone. The child eventually realizes that paternal approval was a myth, a cruel hope never truly available to him.

Most children of disapproving fathers accept mediocrity for themselves. Wouldn't you? If you're going to receive disapproval no matter what you do, wouldn't a general ache of disapproval be better than the sharp pangs of failure? Such a child would rather hold back, achieving only enough to get by, than face Dad's lukewarm reaction or angry dissatisfaction if he fails. Each time such an interaction occurs, the relationship slips back another notch.

Your children want you to be proud of them, Dad. They need your approval. If you respond to their failures with negative, sarcastic, or hurtful statements instead of with words that turn the situation into an opportunity for encouragement, you are paving their path to teenage rebellion—or worse.

Failures often create open-window moments. The wise father seizes these moments to build up his vulnerable child. In the Ezzo household, when the children failed—either in an achievement or a relationship—Anne Marie and Gary attempted to help them find the secret blessing. They often said, "Do you realize the number of adults who have not learned the lesson you've learned today? Do you realize how many people live foolishly because they lack the wisdom you now possess?" Those were not words of condemnation or correction, but of encouragement. They were not meant to dismiss the pain of failure, but to help their children see that out of defeat can come a victory they never expected.

The Ezzos knew their children would be tested again in a similar fashion and that when that day came, they would be ready to face it with wisdom. They would then turn failure into victory. And when that victory came, Dad and Mom would be there to share the joy.

Your middle-years child needs to know that you too have failed and can feel her hurt and disappointment. She needs to be assured that your parent-child relationship is based on neither failure nor success. Please note: It is not the fear of failure itself that holds a child back, but the fear of failing *someone*. Often that someone is Dad. You must give your child reason to trust in a father who will remain loving and accepting, even when she fails.

Dad's Little Notes

How many young fathers wish their dads had written them just one note—something simple and encouraging? Something that ended in three little words: "I love you." It doesn't take much effort to put a little note in your child's lunch box occasionally. Something so small can be immeasurably important to your child. Consider the following letter the Ezzos received.

Dear Gary and Anne Marie,

I am writing to thank you and testify to the truth you imparted to us during last month's conference. I brought my husband to the seminar in the hope that he would be more willing to take a positive role in fathering if he heard things straight from you.

A few days after we returned home we were talking

about fathers leaving notes for the child instead of mom always doing it. (That was something I had been doing for a few months.) My husband agreed to put a note in our seven-year-old boy's lunch box. The next morning he wrote the note and left instructions to place it in the lunch box, which I did. It was just a simple note saying, "Hope you have a nice day at school. See you when I get home. Love, Dad."

Upon our son's return home, he handed me his lunch box as usual. When I opened it, the note was there. He obviously hadn't seen it. So I said, "You missed something in your lunch box today." He took the note and read it, and then, before me, my son broke down and wept. I hugged him and waited a few moments, then asked why he was crying. He replied, "I didn't realize Dad loved me that much."

How can I ever thank you enough for such a priceless moment in the life of our child?

The time invested by this father was probably thirty seconds, but the impact of his thoughtfulness may last a lifetime. The older the child gets, the more he or she needs to hear from Dad in writing.

Take time to write your children a letter at least once a year. Sign it, seal it, and mail it. Your child will realize that the letter he or she holds is from a man unlike any other in the world—Dad. Letters from friends may eventually get thrown out, but Dad's letters will get safely put away. And in the future, during those discouraging moments or perhaps on lonely days, those notes will come out again and again, bringing an assurance of at least one certainty: Dad's love.

Also, Dad, consider signing family Christmas and birthday cards. It doesn't matter how illegible your penmanship is. There is something very special about knowing Dad took a little time to endorse the warm thoughts enclosed in the envelope. Children don't usually question Mom's commitment to the family, but such gestures go far to confirm Dad's devotion.

Take your child's need for encouragement seriously. You know from hindsight that life's disappointments are survivable and that everything usually turns out fine. But your child doesn't know that. Many times a father underestimates a child's sense of urgency. What may seem trivial to you may seem insurmountable to your son or daughter. Listen for the clues. Realize there will be some matters of major importance packaged in an insignificant statement. Seize the opportunity to encourage your child through his or her difficulties by imparting your experience and wisdom.

Routinely Embrace Your Child

Within the family, a gentle hand, a tender hug, a pat on the back, and a good-night kiss all communicate intimacy in a relationship. To hold and be held communicates a vulnerability and closeness that is reserved for trusting members of a family.

There is something very special about Dad's arms. Mom's arms are comforting, but Dad's arms are secure. Neither a child's age nor gender should limit a father's touch. Our children are never too old to be kissed, hugged, or held—never. Even as a full-grown man, Gary would give anything to be held one more time by his own dad, who passed away in 1972.

Think of all the fathers who have the opportunity to hold their children, but don't. Don't be one of those. Go hug your child right now.

Holding your child does more than provide security. It meets special emotional needs that one day will be met by your child's mate. This is particularly critical for fathers of daughters who are beginning to blossom into their womanhood. Many dads unconsciously begin to back away physically when their daughters reach this stage in life. Poor girl! Not only does she have to cope with her changing body, but now, just when she's feeling the most unlovely, her father pulls away from her.

Your daughter is still your little girl. She still needs hugs and kisses. If you fail to communicate your love through your touch, you will leave behind a yearning heart that can be taken captive by anyone willing to give it attention. Don't leave your child open to the affections of the wrong person. Hold your preteen and don't ever stop.

One caveat: The way you tickled and wrestled with your daughter a few years ago may not be the most appropriate form of play for your thirteen-year-old. While a mother teaches a daughter the facts of life, a father communicates a private message to a daughter by what he does and does not do. That message must always work to promote, protect, and preserve the dignity and sanctity of your daughter's developing womanhood.

SUMMARY

Any man can be a father, the bumper sticker goes, but it takes a real man to be a daddy. If you trace every social problem in America today back to its roots, the primary cause has something to do with fatherhood. Gangs are surrogate families for teens whose fathers have left the family—physically and/or emotionally. Teenage girls get pregnant because they're looking for the masculine affection their fathers failed to give. Young people experiment with drugs because they have no strong father at home giving them the tools to resist peer pressure.

Fatherlessness is an epidemic in America. While you can't solve that disease, you can at least work to make your family immune.

BRINGING IT HOME

1. Was your own father a dad worthy of trust? In what ways do you hope to emulate what he did as a father? How do hope to do things differently?

2. What is the one thing that most affects the strength of a father's relationship with his children?

3. What is an open-window moment? Describe one you've had with your middle-years child. Would you do anything differently if you could do it over?

4. Why should fathers verbalize their commitment to their families?

5. Listen to your "little" comments to your child. Do you hear yourself using critical language? Every father can redouble his efforts to build up his child.

6. Give your child a special embrace today. Just take three minutes to hold your child (even if he or she wants to squirm) and express your heartfelt love.

Chapter Thirteen

The Sex Talk I:
Fathers and Sons

Sex is all around us. On billboards, in music, on TV. It doesn't matter what you're selling, sex will sell it for you. You can bet your preadolescent son has noticed.

It is your responsibility, Dad, to have "the talk" with your son. If you don't explain things to him, someone else will. He'll learn a twisted version of it from a dirty magazine somebody brought to school, movies you don't think he has access to, little Sammy's big brother, or Internet sites that would make a vice cop blush.

Your son can easily get information about sex. What you want to give him is accurate, moral information that is consistent with the kind of home you want. If you portray sex as tender intimacy reserved for marriage, you give him defenses against the locker room brag sessions, street-smart bravado, and only-the-good-die-young mentality so prevalent around him.

In our opinion, the sex talk is best done father-to-son and mother-to-daughter. In some cases, of course, this is not possible. If you are a single parent reading this chapter, perhaps you know a loving same-gender relative or family friend who can step in. Or you may sensitively approach the issue with your opposite-gender child. But if possible, keep this talk along gender lines.

LOCKER ROOM OR BATHROOM?

Let's start with an easy topic and ramp up to the main event. There are many external changes taking place in your son's body during the preteen years. Usually around the age of ten or eleven, a boy's body changes require that you give him an education in grooming.

A family we know of with four sons one day realized the bathroom was beginning to take on the odor of a locker room. That was a clear sign that it was time for their eldest son to learn about personal hygiene.

This is a situation that must be handled sensitively. An offhand remark like, "Kid, you don't smell so good," has the potential to evoke shame and embarrassment in a child. So what is the best way to introduce something as basic as the need for deodorant?

To begin with, Dad, recognize that there is no need to be blunt or unkind. Comments like "You stink. Start using some deodorant under your arms," or "I can smell you a mile away. It's time for the stick," threaten the security and trust we talked about in the previous chapter. (Those also will be the words your children will use on their siblings.)

Sensitively educate your son about such matters. Explain the circumstances of physical maturity, including the fact that new sweat glands develop as bodies grow. Show him it's something to be proud of, not ashamed of—a sign that he's entering manhood. Help your preteen understand that he is not the only one experiencing this change and that it happens to everyone during preadolescence.

Explain how sweat attaches to our skin, underarm hair, and clothes and why bathing, changing clothes, and using deodorant are important daily habits.

You may be able to take advantage of a deodorant commercial on TV by making a comment such as: "That guy is using roll-on deodorant. That's what I use, and at the rate you're becoming a man, son, you're going to need your own soon." Then, you can sit back and wait for the questions to arise. Don't worry if none comes right away; your son may simply be processing the comment. In time, however, both his curiosity and need to know will increase.

The practice of self-care and personal hygiene is second nature to adults. For children, however, this is not the case. They must be taught, and gently. As physically maturing children detect new smells and experience other bodily changes, they often feel an over-whelming self-consciousness. Reassure your son that adults have the same problem with perspiration, but they know how to take care of it—just as he will learn to do.

SON, LET'S GO FOR A WALK

We must never forget that as fathers, we play an important part in the shaping of both our sons and daughters' emotional and sexual development. To that end, Dad should give warm embraces and powerful hugs to both daughters and sons, but especially to sons. Though it might seem otherwise when viewed through a cultural lens, a father's touch actually confirms a son's sense of masculinity.

Your preadolescent son needs more than a hug, however. He needs an education about his changing body. Human sexuality is one of the most complex of all human issues. There is much more to preparing your prepubescent son than communicating biological facts. We firmly believe that biological details need a relational and moral context if they are to have any real meaning to children.

But what our society is offering today is something far inferior. The exploitation of young minds for commercial gain encourages premature and distorted views of sexuality. This is certainly true in the case of boys. James Bond is offered as the ideal of masculinity—free to enjoy every woman who comes along, without any consequences or commitment.

Can a father counter such influences? Yes, he can—by teaching and modeling for his son what it means to respect, honor, and appreciate the tenderness of womanhood. The many gestures of kindness you show your wife indelibly set in your son's mind a pattern of thinking and behaving that provides a context in which his sexual awareness can grow.

While girls' needs during puberty are generally addressed in helpful detail in our society, boys' needs are often skimmed over with a few generalizations. "Boys are tough; they adjust just fine," we hear people say. The resulting impression is that girls are somehow more complex than boys. On the contrary—it takes great skill and insight to figure out what's going on in an eleven-year-old boy's head and body.

Because boys do not experience anything that signals the sudden onset of puberty (such as menstruation), many fathers feel no sense of urgency to talk with their sons about the changes about to occur. Add to that the fact that boys are usually two years behind girls in physical and social development, and it's easy to see why "the talk" never takes place. But some talking is necessary.

And don't take the coward's way out, Dad. Don't just put a book on the subject in your son's room when he's at school. Poof, it magically appears. And Dad weasels out of talking about it. An age-appropriate book about sex is a great idea. Your son can look things up for himself. But introduce it to him personally. Hand it to him after "the talk," or, even better, go through it with him.

By keeping your son's sexuality at arm's length, you send the message that you don't want to talk about it, that you aren't available to answer his questions, and that it is not an issue fit for open discussion in the family. In anticipation of the teenage years, you want to be building bridges to your son, not burning them. If he's asking you questions about sex, you at least have a chance to get the truth into the mix of everything else he's hearing.

OF AVIARIES AND HIVES
(THAT'S "THE BIRDS AND THE BEES" TO YOU AND ME)

Of course, teaching your son about life after puberty goes far beyond how to use deodorant. You must also deal with the new and powerful feelings that are beginning to surge through his body.

Explain to your son that according to life's timetable, his body will awaken to entirely new sensations that are good and pleasurable and natural. Instill in him the knowledge that these feelings are to be given full expression only within the context of marriage.

You must decide to what extent you will communicate specific sexual details to your son and how explicit you will be. Will you initiate conversation about self-stimulation? Will you dialogue about the awkward stiffness that comes on a young man as a result of hormone surges at the sight of a pretty girl? Will you warn your son that this phenomenon often happens at the worst times—such as waiting in the lunch line, watching a football game, or standing in front of the class reading a history report? Or will you allow him to make his own personal adjustments? Will you tell him everything now, or just cover chapters 1, 2, and 3 today and do some more next week?

These decisions will be based on family history, the peers with whom your son associates, his social and moral surroundings, the temperaments of both you and your son, and his age. Every family is different, and so is every child. Understand, therefore, that more information is not necessarily better information, but that some information is a must.

The decision of how and what to share is yours. But whatever you choose, it is imperative that you communicate to your son that he is not alone. Make sure he understands that he is not the only one to experience these sensations. Assure him that he is in good company, that all boys his age are in fact experiencing the same feelings and tensions. Perhaps a story from your own puberty would be helpful—if you haven't buried the memories entirely, that is.

As you discuss his growing sexuality, share with him the truth that he, along with all other boys around his age, will soon have the biological capacity to procreate. In addition to whatever details you give about how this actually happens, be sure to emphasize that with that capacity comes a great responsibility. He must learn to properly manage these new feelings and drives.

This is not an easy task for a son to achieve or a father to communicate, but nonetheless the message must get across. At some point your son must come to the place where self-control with purpose overrides the prompting of hormones.

By "self-control with purpose" we mean that man is more than an animal driven by instinctual urges, like the animals of the forest. Man is a moral creature with both the will and capacity to subdue physical urges. "With purpose" speaks to the motive for his self-control. He is not simply suppressing urges because Dad or Mom suggested it, but because he has learned to respect the power to create life. Teaching a son about the dignity of human life goes hand in hand with teaching him about his sexuality.

SUMMARY

Sex education would be much easier if the only thing parents needed to do was live morally and sexually pure lives in front of their children and not have to teach or answer questions. But there are questions of curiosity that come up from time to time, and those questions need answers from a trustworthy parent.

Above all, Dad, you must be available to your son. Sometimes you will initiate the conversation or encourage him to bring questions to you. At other times, your son will bring up a subject. But always, your middle-years son must have the confidence that you will encourage and respect this area of his developing masculinity.

BRINGING IT HOME

1. Why is it better for fathers to talk to sons about sex than for mothers to talk to sons?

2. How did your parents introduce this topic to you? Are you satisfied with how they did it?

3. Go to the bookstore and browse for suitable, age-appropriate books on the subject. Is there one you would feel comfortable going over with your son?

4. Think for a minute how much information you want your son to have about sex right now. As you plan your talk, remember what he is likely to hear from other sources. How can you set him straight on those issues so he doesn't come away with wrong ideas?

5. Can you remember something difficult or embarrassing about your own entrance into puberty? Consider relating that story in order to make your son feel at ease.

Chapter Fourteen

The Sex Talk II:
Mothers and Daughters

By Anne Marie Ezzo

he dreaded talk. Can't you just wait to drag your preadolescent daughter off to some remote corner of your home,
sit her down in the stillness of this anxious moment, and
reveal to her the mysteries of her changing body?

Maybe next week, you say. It's not time, you say. Maybe you're
concerned she'll have far too much to say. Anyway, she has a class
this year that will cover all that. So, you choose to step back and
just be there if she rushes home to share with you over cookies and
milk some tender question about her blossoming body. Not exactly. Nikki, the know-it-all at her school, can fill in there, too, over by
the monkey bars right after lunch.

Time to talk, Mom. Today. Don't get nervous. This isn't the big
talk: the one, the dreaded. That one doesn't exist. There is no simple,
singular talk that can sensitively do justice to your daughter's
emerging womanhood.

First, just talk. Talk about things you like. Laugh about things
you did. Put the kettle on or share the ancient art of making hot

chocolate from scratch. It's time to chat it up with your preadolescent. You'll be setting the stage for comfortable moments of sharing down the road.

Womanhood is a journey. The run and leap approach may leave your tender yearling with cuts and bruises. Step softly. Listen carefully. Stay alert. And brush up on some basic survival skills before you set off.

Confusion is common as preteens start down this path. Many new situations come up, and previously unimportant issues now need your attention. Some will relate to physical changes; others will concern emotional and social development. But one thing remains constant from family to family: Changes are coming, and Mom needs a backpack full of strategies to escape the quicksand and snakebites.

WHERE DOES A MOTHER BEGIN?

As mothers, we enter into our children's middle years with a fairly good track record of knowing what's best. There is no question in our minds about the best jeans to purchase. We have mastered the ideal lunch box and how to stock it full of health and happiness. We carefully select the activities best suited for our kids based on our daily observations of their interests and abilities. Up to this point, we have been carrying out the general management of our children's lives and loving it. After all, this business of family is something of an art form.

But all that changes as your child enters the middle years. This phase of life presents a challenging transition not just for your son or daughter, but for you. Suddenly you're clueless, at least to the kid. What's hip, in, rad, or tight is beyond your comprehension. Because mothers become so proficient at managing, changes that involve letting go and stepping back can be difficult. The woman who has dedicated herself to mothering at the expense of everything else may indeed find this stage traumatic.

As our children move farther and farther away from our direct maternal supervision, we may feel that our influence is being devalued. This is why some moms feel threatened by their children's emergence into the middle years. The daughter who a few short years ago needed Mom for everything is now managing his or her own life and forming independent opinions about the world. This includes opinions about the need for and value of Mom's supervision.

As a mother and grandmother, I have often seen that what we fear about change usually doesn't come to pass. Eventually we adjust to our children's spreading their wings. We must. As we come to appreciate new sides of ourselves, we learn we are not only more adaptable than we previously thought, but far more multidimensional than we imagined. This realization is good for everyone involved. You have already acknowledged that your middle-years child is a changing human being. As you flex with that change, you'll find yourself growing as well.

THE VALUE OF FAMILY

During this time, you need to remember how important you are in your child's world. While outside influences are becoming more of a factor, the greatest influence in a child's life is still her family. Within the family, children develop a sense of who they are, and their parents' compass points them to the direction they will take in life. How a child adjusts to adolescence is often the result of how well (or how poorly) his or her parents adjusted to the many transitions found in the middle years.

Although a family shares a common roof, meals, and love, no two members of the family relate in exactly the same way. Your preadolescent, for example, relates to Mom and Dad as a unit differently than she relates to either parent alone, or in a group of siblings. You as a parent also treat that child differently when you are alone with her than you do when your other children or spouse are present.

As your child moves through preadolescence, both the mother-child and father-child relationship take on new significance. Daughters look to their mothers to model their future role of womanhood. For their part, fathers provide a sounding board on which girls can test their femininity. Your daughter, for example, may love to go shopping with you, but she runs to Dad to show off her new outfit. She does this for a reason: She is measuring his response as a type of masculine gauge. "What does Dad think?" often translates into "What will boys think about me in this dress?"

Parent-child relationships are also highly significant to preadolescent boys. Sons need their mothers to remain the emotional cushion they can fall back on when life gets tough. While a preteen boy may not physically crawl up into Mom's lap for comfort anymore, he will continue to seek that comfort in less direct ways. You may see evidence of this in your son's need for compliments or approval or the desire simply to be near you while you are cooking dinner or going about your daily tasks.

Preteen boys need their fathers to mentor them on their journey into manhood. How your husband treats you during your son's preadolescent years has a profound influence on how he will treat girls.

PREPARING FOR SURVIVAL

We all bring different personal experiences and backgrounds to our mothering. Yet there are certain aspects of womanhood that are constant. The desire to nurture drives us to equip our children to care for their basic personal needs and to provide a model of what it means to run a home. Do not assume they will learn such skills without your influence.

Preparing your children to be self-sufficient is a process. When my own children were quite small, I set several "survival goals" for them. I would recommend this practice to all young moms. By the time my daughters reached thirteen years of age, I wanted them to have a working knowledge of how to run a home. That included the basics of shopping for food and clothing, preparing simple meals, doing laundry, cleaning the house, managing a budget, and even preparing Thanksgiving dinner.

These are some of the survival goals I set for my children. You will certainly have your own list. As I worked with my daughters, however, my thought was simply this, *If something should happen to me, could the girls take care of themselves—and their dad?*

I did not wait until my children were on the verge of their teen years to begin the training. I had a proactive plan that began to take shape when they were very young. As the girls moved into the toddler years, I began to teach them how to sort clothes and put them into baskets. They would often follow me to the washer and observe the process of putting the clothes inside and adding deter-gent. When it came time to hang out the clothes (yes, coming from New England, I actually hung up my clothes), the girls would hand me the items to go on the line. As they grew, each girl learned how to fold clothes and eventually how to put them away. Did all this take extra time? Of course. All training does.

I followed a similar procedure for each skill I wanted them to learn. For example, it was not uncommon for one of the girls to sit on a stool in the kitchen as I cooked. She would observe my actions and, when she was developmentally able, would place the ingredi-ents in the mixing bowl. If she was too young to do it by herself, I would hold her hand as we used the mixer or turned the mixture with a spoon. It was not until the girls were around ten that I was fully confident I could let them use the stove.

Let me make one important clarification here: Domestic duties are not just for girls. Sons should learn the same things daughters do. Practically speaking, that means boys learn to do laundry, vac-uum, wash dishes, iron their own clothes, wash floors, and help Mom hang curtains. If you are the mother of a son, consider your future daughter-in-law. Every son is a husband-in-training. Now's your chance to raise up the ideal husband for some lucky girl.

You and your husband both have a responsibility to help your sons in this area. While more of the actual instruction may fall on your shoulders, your son will follow his father's example. If your husband demonstrates a willingness to help around the house, your son will be much more likely to adopt the same behavior.

The object is to set a goal and to walk your child—boy or girl—through the steps to achieve it. Whether that goal is having the skills to set a formal table, greet an honored guest, or cook a chicken, the process of learning should be initiated early. By the time your son or daughter is a teen, he should be ready to take over the household duties should the need arise. Once your child reaches this level of readiness, he will also be prepared to feed, clothe, and care for himself during the young adult years that lie ahead.

WORDS TO A DAUGHTER

From the beginning of the species, mothers and daughters have shared a unique bond. While a son will break away, a daughter will see herself as joined to her mother by love, feelings, gender, and the powerful ability to bear life.

The impact of the knowledge of that ability is confirmed by one of the most significant events in her life: the beginning of her menstruation. Although our daughters' feelings related to estrogen and progesterone will be unique, their experiences will draw on mutual sympathies and create an unspoken bond of sisterhood.

A preadolescent girl's growth and development can become a source of anxiety and confusion for her. As thirteen-year-old Casey watched her dad swing, twirl, and wrestle with her seven-year-old sister, she sighed. Turning to her mom she said, "I wish I didn't have to grow up anymore."

Casey wanted to put a stop to puberty. Unfortunately, her budding entrance to womanhood had caused her father to stop his familiar play-touch. (Remember that Gary cautioned fathers not to physically back away from their developing daughters.) Now Casey is resistant to change. But this resistance is not the result of a misconceived idea about the process of maturing; it is the result of how her maturation is affecting other relationships. Be aware.

PUBERTY

What is puberty, and when does a child reach it? Scientists tell us that puberty is a phase of physical development, a biological marker that signifies sexual maturity. It is triggered by the hypothalamus, a region located at the base of the brain that regulates the activity of the pituitary gland. The word *puberty* originates from the Latin word, *pubes,* meaning "to become covered, as with hair." At around eleven years of age for girls, pubic hair starts to appear and her breasts begin to develop.

As we stated in chapter 1, hormonal changes in the endocrine system begin in children at approximately age seven, not twelve or thirteen, as is commonly believed. At around nine and a half years, hormonal changes trigger a prepubescent growth spurt in girls. By the time she reaches age fourteen, the average girl will have become twenty-five percent taller than she was at age nine and will have almost doubled her body weight. It is no wonder that girls become more self-conscious about their personal appearance during this rapid growth period.

During this phase of growth my own daughters began to require more sleep at night and after-school naps were not uncommon. Their little cereal dishes of childhood were replaced with Mom-and-Dad-sized bowls. This increased appetite made glandular sense: The hypothalamus was signaling a need for more food so that the body could get enough energy to meet its growing demands. During the middle years, more than ever, moms need to provide nutritional meals and snacks and help their children avoid junk food.

MENSTRUATION

Of all the changes that take place in your daughter during puberty, the onset of monthly menstruation creates the most anxiety. Menstruation is not a gentle, gradual, or leisurely transition. It is a spontaneous event that comes without advance warning from the body. One day your daughter simply discovers that she is bleeding. This can be a source of great fear for her. However, education can significantly reduce your daughter's anxiety.

How can you prepare your daughter for the changes that are about to come, especially for menstruation? From my experience as a nurse, childbirth educator, and most importantly a mother of daughters, I have gathered a few suggestions to help guide your efforts.

1. Realize you have competition.

Even a simple trip to the mall assaults your child's senses. Life-size posters display scantily clothed women, who should have done some shopping themselves before the photo shoot began. These so-called ads may aim to sell clothes, but they really sell much more— at the expense of our children.

Today, our children live in a world of sexual deviancy. Your pre-teen is growing up in a day when sexuality is neither regulated within marriage, nor governed by Judeo-Christian values. Sex is a commodity for sale, and it sells well. Prime-time television exploits it; magazine advertisements profit by it; and young girls are told they can become glamorous by flaunting it. Public discourse constantly bombards our young children with sexual imagery that excites curiosity and stirs the fires within.

Your daughter knows her body is changing and that she is in the throes of new set of emotions and sensations. She also knows that sex has something to do with it. Decide now the standards of sexual morality you want to impart to your child. If sexual purity is critical to you, and I hope it is, will you require this physically? Do you desire to maintain your child's mental purity as well?

Today such notions are considered antiquated and prudish—even dangerous. What does your heart say? Don't base your hopes for your child on what you believe is the norm; base your standards on what you know to be right. Take a stand for your child's moral innocence. The decisions you make now, the environments in which you allow your daughter to be placed, will affect her the rest of her days. Guard well your child's heart. The climate today would have you corrupt it.

2. *Realize the context of your sexual message is already established.*

No conversation about sexuality takes place in a vacuum. Every day, in a number of ways, we communicate sexual messages and values to our sons and daughters. The way a husband and wife respond to each other at the close of the workday will carry a subtle message of sexuality. Do you and your husband kiss at the door? How long do you kiss? Do you hug? How tightly? How do you look at one another? When your parents come by for a visit, do you hug the same way, with the same intensity, and kiss the same way in front of them as you do when they are not present?

Your attitudes toward modesty and acceptable displays of affection have a profound effect on your child's moral development because they set the parameters of acceptable and unacceptable thinking. What you wear around the house (a sheer nightgown or bathrobe) and what you watch on television are just two examples. Parental purity communicates family attitudes that ultimately provide your child with a frame of reference.

Your children are watching you. Over time and in a deep way, you are leaving an impression about sexuality—yours and theirs. It is into this context that you begin to teach your daughters about the changes to come and what they mean physically and morally.

3. Realize Mom is the best person for the job.

No book serves as a substitute for heart-to-heart dialogue between Mom and child. If sex education, and especially a conversation about menstruation, were simply a matter of communicating biological facts, then a book *would* be enough. But female sexuality is much more complex. That is why both a child's mind and heart must be prepared.

On what subject other them sexuality, would we consider the book approach? Imagine your child comes home one day feeling melancholy. When you ask what's wrong, she tells you that life seems pretty dismal. In fact, she's even considered that hers is no longer worth the effort. A friend at school has hinted at some painless ways to end it all. She asks what you think. In response, you hand this lost and confused child a comprehensive book on the subject of teen suicide and consider the matter closed.

Sound ludicrous? For your preadolescent, simply reading a

school-supplied booklet on puberty and emerging sexuality is no more far-fetched. What your child comprehends at this stage has life-shaping, perhaps life-shattering, results. Often books on this subject are written simply to educate. End of story. They sometimes presuppose that critical virtues are present and active in the life of the young reader. Unfortunately the values often are not there. Sex educators can anticipate neither the quantity nor quality of the moral training a home life has fostered.

If the minds and hearts of children have not been prepared properly, even the most nobly conceived book can damage a child by providing information she is not ready to handle. For some children, this newfound knowledge may be the passkey into an enticing new world. Where moral restraint has not been instilled, their understanding breeds an acceptance of unrestricted sexual behavior. A book of information is not a good substitute for a mom who knows her child's heart.

4. Realize there is a timing issue related to your talk.

Biological and sexual information is best shared with children progressively. In truth, there is no such thing as a one-time chat with our daughters. Instead, we engage in a series of talks that culminate in a specific conversation about menstruation. Speak to your daughter with sensitivity, and always seek to preserve her dignity.

Dialogue between mother and daughter can begin around the age of nine. It was around that age that I began to give my own daughters hints about issues of their development. That doesn't mean I withheld information from the girls. I simply began to make reference to changes that were coming. For example, I once purchased deodorant for myself and, for the first time, for my daughter. When she got home, I gave her the product, asked her to put it away, and casually told her she was going to need it soon because her body was about to go through some changes.

This simple comment brought a simple question: "Why?" From there, I was able to approach the topic of her change in a very nonthreatening manner. "One of the signs that you are maturing is the presence of underarm perspiration. That is why teenagers and adults use deodorant. It helps take care of the smell that comes with the sweat, so we are not offensive to other people. There will be more changes to talk about later, but for now you can just put your deodorant away."

That little conversation went a long way. It opened the door for questions, and gave her a jumping-off point for our next conversation, which took place at around age nine and a half.

I know some women who were more technical in their explanations to their daughters. When the window of opportunity came, they approached the subject by discussing how the hypothalamus and pituitary gland regulate the hormones that cause body changes. For these women, a more textbook-type approach worked best.

When my daughters reached nine and a half, I was more direct than before, but still discreet. I started to talk generally about Cassandra, a teenager we knew, remarking that she was beginning to blossom into a beautiful young lady. The kids admired Cassandra, so she became a good role model for them.

The conversation included some specific details about how wonderfully made our bodies are. I explained in simple terms about hormones that cause girls like Cassandra to grow toward womanhood. I told them that, like Cassandra, they too would begin to develop breasts, and I informed them that some hair would begin to appear in their pubic area.

These mother-daughter conversations about menstruation became even more direct when each daughter reached age ten. It was then that they began to notice the early signs of maturation, including the first stages of breast development and pubic hair.

These conversations took some planning on my part. I wrote to one of the many feminine hygiene companies and requested a "starter packet" that I could use to generate discussion with my daughter. The package was very helpful. If you take this same approach, however, be sure to review the box and its contents. Some information may not be appropriate for your daughter. All she needs at this age is basic information about the anatomy as it relates to her menstrual cycle and her personal hygiene.

Why Blood?

For a young girl, perhaps the most confusing aspect of menstruation is the role blood plays in the process. What is the function and purpose of it? At some time during one of your conversations, you should help your daughter put the process of menstruation into perspective by answering these questions.

In the truest biological sense, there are life-sustaining properties within blood. Tell your daughter that once a month, a woman's body places life-sustaining nutrients in the womb in anticipation of conception. These nutrients are contained in the blood. If no child is conceived that month, the blood with all its special "food" will be passed out of the body. Explain that this begins what is commonly referred to as menstruation, or a period.

As a mother, you will direct the conversation and, based on your daughter's age, moral and sexual awareness, and ability to process all that she is hearing, determine how extensively you will answer questions. But at some point, this information will be helpful. If your child never knows the answer to the question, "Why blood?" the entire process will continue to be nothing more than a mysterious, confusing nuisance she must live with every month.

Early in your first conversations your daughter might say, "Oh, I know all about periods. Becky told me it happened to her sister at school." Do not let that statement go unchallenged. Follow it up with, "I'm sure you have a general knowledge about this, but do you know about ovulation, or the mild cramps that may accompany your period?" Ask questions. Do not end this conversation without understanding what she knows as distinguished from what she thinks she knows.

It is important also that you not assume that each daughter will receive the news in the same way. One daughter may offer an emphatic response like, "That's not going to happen to me!" To this, you may gently respond, "Yes, in fact, whether you like it or not, this happens to all women. It is part of life, and you will adjust to these changes just as all women before you have adjusted." Another daughter may receive the same talk with great anticipation and excitement about growing up. There is no right or wrong response in these two examples, but both need to be directed and understood.

One final warning: Do not feel obligated or pressured into sharing sexual information beyond the basics of menstruation. Your daughter at this age does not need to know about the intimate details surrounding marital intercourse. What needs to be said on that subject will come later as she moves into moral maturity and preparation for marriage. Certainly, answer whatever questions she comes to you with, but keep the answers age-appropriate and related to the changes in her body.

5. Realize the importance of follow-up.

Keep in mind there will always be teaching opportunities before and after menstruation starts. Commercials serve as good starting points. If you and your daughter are watching television together and you see an advertisement for a feminine hygiene product, use that opportunity to discuss the merits of that particular product in hopes of triggering further discussion about her menstruation.

Once her cycle starts, help her understand that "normal" is what is normal for her. While many have a period every twenty-eight days, some go longer and some shorter. Make sure your daughter understands that irregular cycles, particularly initially, are not uncommon. That fact will allow you to speak further to the issue of preparedness and personal hygiene.

It is likely that conversations with your daughter will sooner or later lead to the question of Dad. "Does Dad know about these things?" I believe that fathers should be told when their daughters begin menstruation. Your husband needs to know, not because he will serve as an advisor in such matters, but because he must be made aware of the need to be sensitive to his daughter with regard to the many physical and emotional changes taking place.

Girls feel more comfortable talking with mothers about the

intimate details of menstruation and their developing bodies. Dad does not have to be part of this conversation, and usually he is not welcome. That is okay.

Mothers have told me how their daughters recoiled at the thought of Dad's involvement in any conversation about menstruation. Young girls believe their fathers could not possibly understand these things. And they are right to some extent. Emotionally and experientially, most men are limited in their understanding of menstruation.

Keep Dad informed and encourage him in his role as a loving and dedicated father. Continually remind him to hug his daughter and to affirm her developing femininity. But gently tell him not to assume that he is an equal voice in this matter and one that she will appreciate hearing from. He is not.

Finally, when your daughter starts to menstruate, *do not* announce it at the dinner table, your weekly coffee klatch, or to the neighbor next door. If you do that, you may destroy the trust and confidence your daughter has in you. There are enough challenges in a preadolescent's life. Broadcasting the onset of her period will only complicate matters for her—and you. Be sensitive to this. This is an issue between daughter and mother. Leave it there.

6. Realize that your daughter will have concerns.

Think back to the questions you had when you first learned about or began menstruation. You may or may not have brought your concerns to your mother, but you do want your daughter to be able to come to you.

In all likelihood, your daughter will have questions that reflect the very same concerns you had as a young girl. These concerns can be greatly reduced through proactive guidance. By being aware of them, you will be able to support and understand your daughter more effectively during this difficult phase of life. Here are five of the most common concerns young girls have regarding menstruation.

1. Everyone at school will know I have my period.

Your daughter's increased self-consciousness and heightened sensitivity to her own body are what trigger this concern. After she begins menstruating, she will notice that in addition to the increased perspiration that naturally occurs with the development of sweat glands, body secretions and the passing blood will also give off a slight odor.

The solution, of course, is basic hygiene. Let your daughter know she will make it through her period without detection if she routinely changes her pads, takes daily showers, and when she is ready, considers the use of feminine hygiene products.

2. It can strike at any time.

It is frightening for a young girl to know that she may begin bleeding at any moment. You can help reassure your daughter by explaining the concept of cycles. While there are charted average norms, let your daughter know that menstruation cycles vary from woman to woman. Your daughter needs to understand that "normal" for her is whatever her cycle proves to be. Over time, she will establish regular and predictable patterns. Predictability then leads to the three "Ps": *planning* activities, *preparing* for surprises, and *preventing* accidents.

3. I will bleed to death.

Prior to the onset of menstruation, your daughter's only experience with bleeding has been related to injury. It is natural for her to wonder how much blood can be lost before bleeding becomes life-threatening. Reassure your child that while it may feel like she is losing a lot of blood, blood loss during menstruation is insignificant—usually less than one-half ounce—and is blood that is designed to be lost. This is also the time to teach the importance of proper nutrition, which is essential for the body to maintain proper fluid balances, including the production of red blood cells.

4. It's going to hurt.

Menstrual cramps, mild to severe, are a fact of life. However, we live in a day when over-the-counter medication is available to help a woman through the first days of her period. Help your daughter understand her analgesic choices.

Also, please be aware that you have a profound influence on how your daughter responds to menstrual cramps. Remember, every woman responds to pain and discomfort differently. Be careful how you communicate your own experience and responses. If you take to bed once a month, do not assume that your daughter's body will necessitate the same. On the other hand, if you are blessed with mild or no cramping, do not assume your daughter's physiology will grant her the same benefits.

5. I can't do anything or go anywhere when I'm on my period.

It is true that menstruation may cause enough discomfort to occasionally curtail a particular physical activity. However, menstruation in and of itself will not prevent your daughter from participating in gym class, swimming, or other sports and social activities that she enjoys. Reassure her that though she will need to make some adjustments, she can and will enjoy life just as much as she has before.

SUMMARY

No matter how many helpful talks you have with your daughter, how many concerns you alleviate, or how conscientious you are as a parent, she will experience some anxious moments. This is inevitable. However, you can ease your daughter's tension by nurturing an open, loving, and understanding relationship with her.

It is your job, Mom, to communicate the facts as your daughter needs them; to be interested, sympathetic, and ready to help when called upon; and to demonstrate your confidence in her ability to face these incredible life changes. Above all, both you and your daughter's father must realize that menstruation is another middle-years transition she has to experience. Through this rite of passage, she will leave behind the protected and sheltered world of childhood and begin a new journey to the privileges and responsibilities of womanhood.

Once your daughter begins to blossom into womanhood, she needs a good friend more than anything. In fact, the definition of a friend will shift from someone to play with to someone to talk to and share life with. Moms need to be such friends to their children. Talk. Spend special quiet time sharing ideas. Build now that bridge of trust.

BRINGING IT HOME

1. What are the changes experienced by moms and daughters, and what difficulties do they raise?

2. When does a child reach puberty?

3. What is wrong with just giving your child a book about sexuality and leaving it at that?

4. When should you begin to explain to your children about the changes taking place in their bodies?

5. Why is it important to have progressive conversations, and not just a one-time talk?

Happy Landings

O h, the joys of parenthood. Our children delight us with their laughter and humor, surprise us with their imaginations, and amaze us with their perception. Through their growing sense of wonder, they renew Mom and Dad's sense of adventure. Through their continual dependence on our care, they make us feel vital. More than that, with their tender smiles and warm hugs, they make us feel *loved*.

Oh, the frustrations of parenthood. Our children have a knack of saying the wrong thing at the wrong time in front of the wrong people. They throw our orderly world into disarray. When we plan an event weeks in advance, that is the exact day they get sick. It seems they track in mud only after the floor is washed and stain only their new clothes. They humble us in public and make us feel like failures in private. This, too, is parenthood.

There is no avoiding this truth: Parenting is a challenge. And the challenge only increases as children grow and their needs become more complex. As parents we naturally want to meet as many of those needs as possible. But while striving to do so, we must be careful not to attempt to meet them in our own strength.

If this is true, whose strength *can* we rely upon? The authors of a best-selling book? Our children's teachers? The couple next door? As helpful as these resources may be, they are not sufficient in and of themselves. If we place our confidence in our own abilities or the abilities of others, we will be too stressed out, too tense, and too anxious to enjoy the parenting process or, more tragically, our children.

Moms and dads, we urge you to settle this in your mind now: You will never have perfect children. None of us will. This is true in part because there is no such thing as a perfect parent, regardless of how many resources are made available to us. However, God's grace takes up the slack of our failures. That's because God knows us and our children so well. He sees us in moments of bliss and frustration. He hears our prayers and sees our smiles and our tears. It is a wonderful gift to have someone who knows the best and worst about us and loves us anyway. More than anything else we have shared with you in these pages, this final truth supersedes them all: With the grace of God on your side, you can enjoy your children now—and forever. Find God and you will find His grace.

Here's hoping your little Mars lander makes it safely to the surface.

Gary Ezzo, M.A.
Robert Bucknam, M.D.

Index

More Parenting Resources

On Becoming Babywise

Coming with the applause of over two million parents and twice as many babies worldwide, *On Becoming Babywise* provides a prescription for responsible parenting. The infant management plan offered by Ezzo and Bucknam successfully and naturally helps infants synchronize their feeding/waketime and nighttime sleep cycles. The results? You parent a happy, healthy and contented baby who will begin sleeping through the night on average between seven and nine weeks of age. Learning how to manage your newborn is the first critical step in teaching your child how to manage his life.

On Becoming Babywise II

This series teaches the practical side of introducing solid foods, managing mealtimes, nap transitions, traveling with your infant, setting reasonable limits while encouraging healthy exploration and much more. You will learn how to teach your child to use sign language for basic needs, a tool proven to help stimulates cognitive growth and advance communication.

On Becoming Pre-Toddlerwise

Between the ages of twelve and eighteen months, a pretoddler is on a one-way track to the future. This is a growth phase made-up of tiny transitions linking the fading babyhood days with the up coming toddlerhood months. It is a time when your child is in neither. *On Becoming Pretoddlerwise* deals with a specific right of passage and the corresponding challenges parents will face.

On Becoming Toddlerwise

By eighteen months of age, the child emerges into a period of life know affectionately as the Toddler Years. How ready are you for this new experience? The toddler years are the learning fields and you need a trustworthy guide to take you through the unfolding maze of your child's developing world. *On Becoming Toddlerwise* is a tool chest of workable strategies and ideas that multiplies your child's learning opportunities in a loving and nurturing way. This resource is as practical as it is informative.

On Becoming Pottywise for Toddlers

Potty training doesn't have to be complicated and neither should a resource that explains it. *On Becoming Pottywise for Toddlers* looks to developmental readiness cures of children as the starting point of potty training. Readiness is primary perquisite for successful training according to best selling authors, Gary Ezzo and Pediatrician Robert Bucknam. While no promise can be made, they can tell you that many moms successfully complete their training in a day or two, some achieve it literally in hours. This resource is filled with time test wisdom, workable solutions and practical answers to the myriad of questions that arise during training.

On Becoming Preschoolwise

Who can understand the mind of a preschooler? You can! Know that above all else, a preschooler is a learner. His amazing powers of reasoning and discrimination are awakened through a world of play and imagination. The growth period between ages three and five years is all about learning, and *On Becoming Preschoolwise* is all about helping parents create the right opportunities and best environment to optimize their child's learning potential. From teaching about the importance of play to learning how to prepare a preschooler for the first day of school, from organizing your child's week to understanding childhood fears and calming parental anxiety, sound advice and practical application await the reader.

On Becoming Childwise

Equip yourself with more than fifteen Childwise principles for training kids in the art of living happily among family and friends. Foster the safe, secure growth of your child's self-concept and worldview. *On Becoming Childwise* shows you how to raise emotionally balanced, intellectually assertive, and morally sensible children. It's the essential guidebook for the adventurous years from toddler to grade-schooler!

On Becoming Teenwise

Why do teenagers rebel? Is it due to hormones, a suppressed primal desire to stake out their own domain, or a natural and predictable process of growth? To what extent do parents encourage or discourage the storm and stress of adolescence? *On Becoming Teenwise* looks at the many factors that make living with a teenager a blessing or a curse. It exposes the notions of secular myth and brings to light the proven how-to applications of building and maintaining healthy relationships with your teens. Whether you worry about your teen and dating or your teen and drugs, the principles of *On Becoming Teenwise* are appropriate and applicable for both extremes and everyone in between. They do work!